Discovering
The Black Isle

Discovering
The Black Isle

DOUGLAS P. WILLIS

JOHN DONALD PUBLISHERS LTD
EDINBURGH

In Memoriam
Francis Millington Synge
Doctor of Trinity College, Dublin, and good friend

ISBN 0 85976 263 7

Phototypeset by Newtext Composition Ltd, Glasgow.
Printed in Great Britain by Bell & Bain Ltd,
Glasgow.

Preface

Long before the opportunity arose to live and work in the Black Isle, I had come to know it as a place of rich character. Now, after years of living here, the attraction is undiminished. At the same time, I have become aware of the strong interest shown in the area both by local folk and by the many hundreds of visitors who venture into the Black Isle each year. I hope that this book may go some way towards filling an oft-expressed need for background information on the area.

There is such a thing as personality of place, that undefinable thing which sets an area apart from all others and gives it its own distinctiveness. The Black Isle is blessed with a personality that is rich and rewarding for those who would seek to know it better.

But we live in an age of change, an age intent on applying the stamp of uniformity. The individual identity of place is everywhere under threat, and we can be grateful that the Black Isle has maintained its distinctive character for so long. The planners charged with decision-making in development and change at the present time bear a heavy responsibility in ensuring that the distinctiveness and attraction are not whittled away. Landscape, countryside – call it what you will – is a resource that needs sympathetic and wise handling.

In the chapters which follow, I have not attempted to produce a step-by-step guide along walks or to places of interest. To do so, I feel, would be to rob the reader of that sense of satisfaction which I have myself experienced in discovering the many facets of the Black Isle. Rather, I hope that this book may be the means of helping the reader towards an enjoyable, personal discovery of a fascinating place.

A book of this type could not have been written without the help of knowledgeable local people. I owe a debt of gratitude to many farming friends, but especially to Alasdair Cameron of Wellhouse, and to the Holm family of Easter Ferryton who have been generous in sharing both information and hospitality. I am grateful also to the Black Isle Farmers' Society for allowing access to their minute books for detail on the history of the Black Isle Show, and to David Watt, Editor of the *Ross-shire Journal,* who kindly made available files of the newspaper from last century.

Information on Avoch came in rich measure from Sandy Jack, Sandy Leitch, Hugh Patience and his uncle, Alexander Macleman, who knew the place in the days of sail. I thank them for their help.

I must record a special debt of gratitude to my wife and fellow geographer, Catherine, for her constant encouragement throughout the writing of this book.

Countless other folk have contributed over the years to my knowledge of the Black Isle, but I confess that it suffers from many limitations still.

Am Fasgadh,
Fortrose

Contents

CHAPTER 1
Setting the Scene

Eilean Dubh. The Black Isle. The name conjures up a vision of a place dark in appearance, some island place removed by water. In the past, this would have been no bad description. Now, two modern bridges link it with the land mass of the Highlands, but until their construction the Black Isle was definitely insular, and from a distance could look decidedly dark.

In reality, the Black Isle is not an island at all, but a peninsula. Firmly joined to the Highlands by a narrow neck of land at its western edge, it is a finger of fertile farmland pointing eastwards towards the North Sea. To the north is the Cromarty Firth, and beyond its tidal waters the distant hills and straths of Easter Ross. To the east and south lie the Moray Firth, the Inverness or Inner Firth, and the Beauly Firth, three interconnecting inlets of the sea, but each possessing its own different character.

Setting the geographical limits of the Black Isle is therefore no difficult task on all but the west side. No enclosing range of hills, no convenient river course exists there as a natural defining line, instead it is the route of the old A9 road, along with a short stretch of the Ross-Inverness boundary near Beauly which serves as the western limit.

The low lying firthlands which surround the Black Isle have provided a good reward for the generations who have tilled their productive soils. But the higher, interior ridge of the Mulbuie was a different matter. Where vast stands of conifers now grow, the ridge was once a great expanse of moor where coveys of grouse shared their heathery home with the folk who came to cast peats for winter fires.

But why Black? The name seems such a contradiction when set against the familiar descriptions of the peninsula as a green and fertile place, totally different in character from the niggardly hill lands to the west.

Ask in the Black Isle, and you will almost certainly be offered the theory that it is because of the appearance of the place on

1

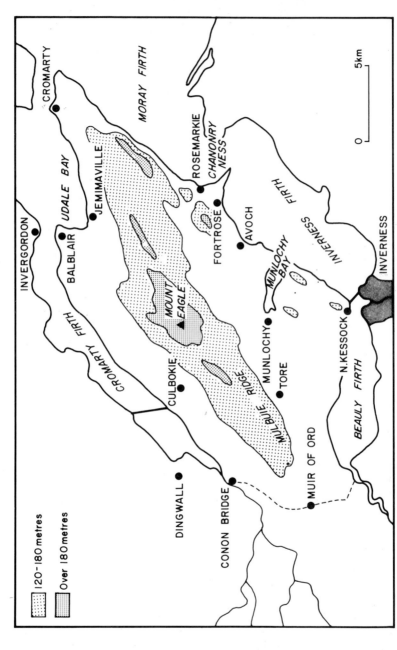

Black Isle – Map of relief and settlement, showing the central Mulbie Ridge and the surrounding villages, each of which retains its own individuality.

snowy winter days. When the hill lands all around are draped in a white blanket, they say, the lower lying Black Isle stands out in dark, striking contrast.

A few folk will offer a less prosaic suggestion, invoking an explanation from the ancient past. Since the name of St Duthac is linked with many spots within the peninsula, might not the Gaelic Eilean Dubh refer not to a black isle at all, it is argued, but to a corrupted Gaelic form of Duthac's Isle?

Personally, I am inclined towards neither of these. The geographer in me favours an alternative for which there appears to be abundant supporting evidence. Hugh Miller, whose name will become familiar in the ensuing pages, grew up in Cromarty and often made the journey westwards through the peninsula in the early part of last century. In his writings, he unfailingly refers to the central Mulbuie Ridge, which he frequently traversed, as dark, bleak or black.

Other writers describe this once vast tract of moorland in equally dismal terms. At the same time, it should be remembered that in an earlier age, the pattern of farmlands was a decidedly peripheral one around the peninsula. In other words, a fringe of green land encircling a long and dominating black core. In this striking pattern of contrast, then, may lie an answer to the question so frequently asked.

Whatever the origins of the name may be, the Black Isle has long enjoyed a reputation as a fertile farming place, and that is how it will inevitably strike the first time visitor. It is a reputation born out of a favourable combination of relief, soil, climate and human endeavour. Unlike the grudging hills to the west, the lie of the land and the covering soils set comparatively few limits to farming activity. And in contrast to the wetter west, the climate is a dry one. Indeed, the Black Isle lies within a part of Britain which enjoys some of the lowest annual rainfall amounts. It is within this favourable geographical context that the Black Isle has gained its reputation as a productive farming area.

It would be a mistake, however, to assume that all interest has been removed from the face of the land with the farming improvements. On the contrary, the Black Isle's crowning glory is its rich patchwork countryside of farmland and intervening trees. The pattern of landscape as we see it in the Black Isle today is essentially the outcome of the long inter-relationship of man and the land. To some extent it is a lowland landscape in a Highland context, but the place is undeniably Highland in location, past history and present outlook.

Beneath the veneer that is the human landscape lie the foundations of the land itself – the rocks which extend the history of the peninsula back beyond the centuries of human presence to the vastly different conditions which prevailed many millions of years ago. At the same time, it should not be forgotten that there is also an important living dimension to the Black Isle scene, giving the peninsula a rich living landscape of farmland, forest and firth.

Compared with the aeons of time when the foundations of the land were being formed, the timescale of man's presence may seem short indeed. Yet, from the days of the shadowy folk who raised up the stone cairns and other lasting memorials of their presence to the days of the present generation who live and work in the place, the Black Isle has seen enormous change. The legacy is as much the whole face of the countryside itself as the individual cairns, castles and other more obvious historical remains which dot its surface.

Tangible reminders of the individual folk who wrought that change may be difficult to identify, but in the quietness of the Black Isle's kirkyards the names of later generations endure on lichened grave slabs shaped from local sandstone. It was this same stone that raised up cathedral and country kirk alike, and the area certainly retains a rich heritage of church foundations.

Echoes of the past are abundantly present in today's landscape, and the Black Isle will amply repay the visitor intent on seeking out its varied history. Sometimes it is a living echo, as in the annual summer show of the Black Isle Farmers' Society. At this long-established event, farmers gather from all corners of the countryside, as their forbears have done for a century and a half before them, to show off the best in livestock and argue over the judge's placings of the prize tickets. In the Fair of St Boniface, the cathedral green of Fortrose yearly comes alive, as it did centuries ago, when the townsfolk honoured the feast day of their saint and had a rare old time on the strength of it.

All that was a long time ago, in an age when the Black Isle

Looking south-west along the cliff-bound edge of the Black Isle peninsula. In the far distance lies the trench of the Great Glen whose fault-line has determined the shape of the coastline.

may as well have been an island, for the main communication was by water. Ferry crossings, not roads, linked the peninsula to the outside world. In time, as road transport improved, most of the ferry services came to an end. But the Black Isle's sense of insularity was to continue right into the 1980s, when Kessock Ferry at last gave way to Kessock Bridge.

Today, the peninsula is connected to the outside world as it never was before, and those new links inevitably mean change, a change that is becoming increasingly evident in the villages. Yet the Black Isle villages remain places of rich character, where days of the past are strongly recalled in buildings of the present.

Each of the Black Isle settlements has had its own individuality. On the western flank, Muir of Ord was the focus of old drove ways, a market centre and railway junction. Conon Bridge stood at the lowest bridging point for crossing the river. Culbokie, now a growing residential settlement, anciently enjoyed the status of burgh and was the venue for an important fair. Jemimaville and Charleston (now joined with

5

North Kessock) were conceived as tiny estate villages and named in honour of members of the land-owning families. North Kessock itself was the important ferry crossing point, while Munlochy has modestly fulfilled the role of rural service centre.

Fortrose was born out of the old Chanonry of Ross, the cathedral settlement which once dominated Black Isle life. Nearby Rosemarkie, the epitome of the country village, enjoyed a satisfying self-sufficiency which persisted over many generations. By contrast, Avoch's life revolved around the fishing, while the colourful speech of its fisher folk has surprised generations of visitors. And, most atmospheric of all, Cromarty has long lived with its faded grandeur and strong sense of the past in its many fine old buildings.

Cromarty gave to the world much of the writings of Hugh Miller, northern naturalist and pioneer of the science of geology, for it was in that pleasant corner that Miller grew up and formed so many of his ideas. Miller was acutely aware of the environment around him, but he had a sense, too, of the peninsula's store of folklore and local belief, a store that probably owed its richness in no small measure to the insularity of the place in the past.

In the Black Isle of today, the visitor will find a countryside of absorbing interest and visual attraction. But it is a place, too, with a strong sense of continuity with days gone by, a place where the strands of past and present are closely interwoven.

CHAPTER 2
Rocks and Ice Age Remains

In understanding scenery, the past is invariably the key to the present. The Black Isle is no exception, for its foundations are deeply rooted in its geological history. Hard old rocks of the Moinian and Lewisian series, which are widespread throughout the North-west Highlands, outcrop also along the eastern edge of the Black Isle from the shore rocks beyond Rosemarkie to the high South Sutor of Cromarty.

The processes of weathering and erosion have shaped the peninsula's coastal cliffs out of these ancient metamorphic rocks. Metamorphic literally means changed, and the power of ancient heat and pressure in creating that change is demonstrated in the contorted patterns of the gneiss and other metamorphic rocks which outcrop along the shore. A short distance inland from Rosemarkie, a large disused roadside quarry is a reminder that this stone was once in demand as a

The ancient metamorphic rocks which outcrop along the eastern coast illustrate the effects of powerful compression in the past.

local source of road metalling. And further along the coast, at the South Sutor of Cromarty, the massive gun emplacements of wartime were given a firm foundation in the hard rock, guarding the narrows of the firth and facing across towards the matching North Sutor cliffs.

But these ancient Highland rocks have had only limited influence in shaping the landscape. The most widespread basis of the scenery is in the much younger, sedimentary rocks of Middle Old Red Sandstone age. In a geological sense, age is decidedly relative, however, and these less ancient strata are actually hundreds of millions of years old.

By an irony of geological history, the rocks which form the central backbone of the Black Isle peninsula are the last remnants of the bottom of a syncline, a kind of saucer-shaped rock formation. The higher, outer edges have long since been eroded away. This elongated, and now largely forested, Mulbuie Ridge reaches a maximum elevation of 256 metres at Mount Eagle, the highest point in the Black Isle, crowned by a towering television transmitter.

We can only speculate on the conditions which resulted in the formation of the Black Isle sandstones, but geologists paint a picture of shallow waters into which sediments were deposited by inflowing streams. Close inspection of the face of the sandstone blocks used in buildings throughout the Black Isle will reveal details of water current markings which recall these ancient stream flows.

There are variations in colouring, too, suggesting that the deposits which make up the rock came from different sources. Sometimes there is a gradation of particle size from fine sand grain to coarse grit, a reminder that in the distant geological past, as now, weather conditions and stream flow might vary considerably. This is best seen in the rock called conglomerate which must have been born out of turbulent water conditions. Once popularly known as 'pudding stone', this much harder rock was thought to resemble an old-fashioned fruit pudding in its striking mixture of rounded stones set into a fine sandy matrix.

Where the conglomerate occurs, it reveals pebbles of grey gneiss set into a background of fine-grained rock, giving the mixture a strong resistance to erosion. As a result, the southern flank of the Black Isle is marked by a series of prominent hills, including the Ord Hill at Kessock and Ormond Hill near Avoch. The same rock type is responsible also for the craggy outline of Craigiehowe at the entrance to Munlochy Bay.

Because of its highly uneven texture, the conglomerate could not be employed as a building medium. By contrast, the Black Isle sandstones enjoyed a great reputation as a building material. The red sandstone magnificence of Fortrose Cathedral was shaped from blocks hewn from quarries some miles to the west, and the elegant merchants' houses of Cromarty speak no less eloquently of the skills of the masons who worked the local stone to perfection.

At one time, the peninsula was dotted in quarries. Hugh Miller of Cromarty began his working life as a stonemason, extracting rock from a local quarry, and progressing from this humble start to an intensive study of the Old Red Sandstone that was to bring the character of the Black Isle rock to a world-wide audience through his writings.

Some of the sandstone strata which Miller studied with such interest contain so many fossil remains that they are termed fish beds. They outcrop only in a few places, for example along the shore at Cromarty and Eathie. The abundant fossil remains within these fish beds suggest warm waters during the Devonian geological era, where oxygen-starved fish gasped their last in evaporating shallows.

Not far from the Black Isle, these same geological conditions were to bring fame and fortune to Strathpeffer, transforming it in the railway age from quiet village to bustling Victorian spa. The water which percolates through foetid fish beds was quaffed in quantity at the elegant little pump room near the village square. After its sojourn among the ancient fish remains, the Strathpeffer spa water took on a distinctive quality – not to mention smell – which was believed to have great therapeutic properties.

Further geological interest is added by a small outcrop of even younger sedimentary rock. Below the Eathie cliffs, the falling tide exposes water-washed beds of soft black shales. These belong to the Jurassic era, and to the same series of rocks which outcrop along the coastline of Easter Ross. They also occur further north still, at Brora on the east coast of

Sutherland, where they yield a soft coal which was mined until recent times.

The Eathie shales contain abundant fossil remains, particularly of coil-like ammonites. These beautifully formed creatures once swam in shallow waters, their shells settling among the deposits of the sea bed when they died. In time, the muddy bottom sediments in which they lay became hardened into the mudstones or shales of today. The small ammonite fossils are easy to spot since they are white, and stand out prominently against the background of flaky black shale in which they are set.

The hard, bullet-like remains of another swimmer also occur in the Eathie shale. Belemnites would, in its day, have been a creature akin to the present day cuttlefish. Its soft parts have not been fossilised, but the hard interior has been preserved as an intriguing, bullet-like form. Country folk once regarded these curious objects with awe, believing that they were thunderbolts, and that they possessed magical power.

In the same place, an easily broken, bluish limestone occurs as nodules which, when split open, sometimes reveal well-preserved ammonite fossils. In fact, the Jurassic beds of Eathie and East Sutherland have furnished geologists with an extremely rich assortment of fossil plant and animal remains from ancient waters decidedly warmer than those which wash the Black Isle shores today.

But rock type has not been the sole factor in shaping the Black Isle peninsula. Two dramatic events, the one tectonic, the other climatic, have had dramatic effects on the scenery. To understand the former, it is necessary to study a map of northern Scotland. On this, the faulted outline of the Great Glen can be traced as a diagonal gash across the face of the land. Earth forces on a cataclysmic scale once wrenched this northern land apart, creating the great trench of Glen More in which Loch Ness lies, and providing the deep and dark water conditions in which a monster might lurk.

The same geological accident also furnished the great civil engineer, Thomas Telford, with an opportunity for east-west canal construction which otherwise would not have existed. The entrance to Telford's Caledonian Canal may be clearly seen across the Beauly Firth from the A9 as the road enters the

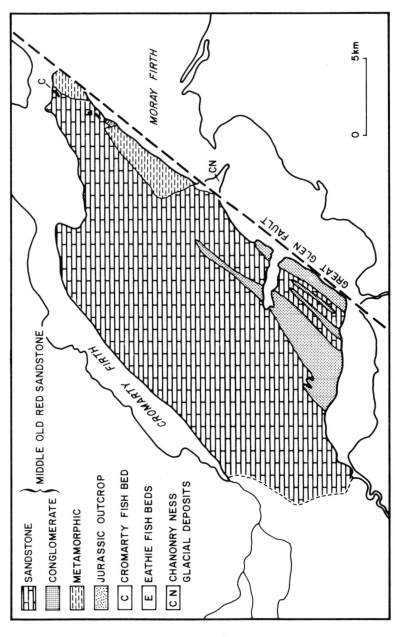

Geology of the Black Isle, showing the widespread occurrence of Old Red Sandstone rocks and the prominent line of the Great Glen Fault.

Black Isle by way of the Kessock Bridge.

When this fault line is traced beyond the Great Glen, it can be noted as the major shaping agent of the whole Black Isle coastline from North Kessock to the South Sutor. Indeed, its influence on the structure of northern Scotland extends well beyond the Black Isle, for it also affects the shape of the Easter Ross coast.

In the Black Isle, the straight edge of this fault-guided coastline is broken only by the inlet of Munlochy Bay and the protrusion of Chanonry Ness. Munlochy Bay itself may owe its origin to stresses emanating from the Great Glen faulting, and the coastal rocks along the line of the fault bear marks of the change which accompanied this dramatic interlude in the area's geological past. For example, the sandstone is so altered in places that farmers refer to it as the 'rotten rock'.

Earth movements connected with the fault line have actually continued into recent times. Several strong earth tremors were experienced in the Inverness area during the 19th century, and one strong shake was reported in a local newspaper as causing 'not a little alarm' to the good folk of the burgh of Dingwall. An exceptionally strong tremor in September 1901 was reckoned to have its epicentre on the fault line close to Inverness, and the effects of the shock waves were felt in the Black Isle and throughout the north.

The occurrence of this line of weakness in the Earth's crust had to be carefully considered when plans were drawn up for the bridging of the Kessock narrows, to link the Black Isle with Inverness. Lengthy underwater foundation works were followed by the construction of a suspension bridge incorporating hydraulic buffers to guard against the effects of any future earth movements.

Spectacular though the effects of the Great Glen Fault may have been on the shaping of the Black Isle, they are confined to its eastern flank. The climatic deterioration which resulted in the Ice Age had a much more widespread influence throughout the whole peninsula. The Black Isle was not high enough to nurture its own ice cap during glacial times. It did not, therefore, suffer the erosion which so obviously scalloped the side of distant Ben Wyvis. Nevertheless, the effects of glaciation were clearly imprinted on the face of the land.

The characteristic Black Isle landscape of farmland, firth and forest is illustrated in the view from Knockmuir Farm towards Ormond Hill. The linear form of the village of Avoch emphasises the presence of the raised beach.

Huge deposits of boulder clay, derived from the break-down of surfaces traversed by the ice, blanket the landscape. Here and there may be picked out the rounded swells of glacial deposition, especially when evening light throws them into more obvious relief. Sometimes they impose local limitations on cultivation, and recall the much larger drumlins which pepper the landscape of South-west Scotland.

But it was perhaps the wasting of the ice as the climate improved that had the most obvious influence. Around Muir of Ord to the west, vast quantities of sands, gravels and pebbles were flushed out of the glacial deposits by melting ice water. Gradually they were spread in a great flat plain of material called outwash.

This unpromising outwash material may have reduced the farming potential of the Muir of Ord area, but it did provide a well-drained stance for the Highland cattle drovers of old and for the modern Black Isle Show. On many occasions, when the weather has not looked too kindly upon the day of the summer show, the organisers and stockmen have had cause to be grateful to those ancient spreads of gravel and pebbles which have furnished them with such an excellent dry site despite the deluges.

With rising temperatures, the ice began to waste away, slowly retreating into the high ground whence it had come. Vast spreads of ground moraine were left behind as a legacy of glacial times, and incorporated into it were huge blocks of 'dead ice'. In time, these slowly melted, allowing ground subsidence to occur. The circular depressions which resulted are widespread at the Muir of Ord end of the Black Isle. These kettle holes are now either damp and reedy hollows surrounded by productive farmland, or else water-filled depressions. An obvious example is one beside the Black Isle Show site which has been transformed from an unsightly rubbish dump into a pleasant picnic spot.

In recent years, geographers have deduced much about the actions of the ice when it blanketed the northern landscape. Of particular interest in the Black Isle is the occurrence of several protrusions of land into the Inverness Firth. Chanonry Ness is easily the most obvious of these. Not surprisingly, local folk had their own explanation for this curious feature. It was formed, they said, by a wizard intent on bridging the narrows across the firth. To be more precise, it was the work of an industrious band of fairy folk which he had assembled for the mammoth task. It seems that great progress was being made on this ambitious engineering work when some unthinking passer-by wished them 'God speed'. At once, the spell was broken and the workers fled, leaving it to the bridge engineers of the 1980s to effect a firth crossing.

So much for the folklore account. The geographer's explanation of this great afterthought of nature tucked on to the fault line is less colourful, but none the less intriguing. Chanonry Ness is considered to be the remains of a gigantic moraine that marked the furthest progress of a tongue of ice which moved down from the high ground during a late readvance.

The other portion can easily be seen from Chanonry Point. It is the huge mass of ground that dominates the coastal village of Ardersier at the opposite side of the firth. In fact, a good perspective on this part of the firth and its origins may be had

Once believed to be the work of a wizard and a band of fairy workers, Chanonry Ness is the sea-worked remnant of a gigantic Ice Age moraine.

from outwith the Black Isle completely, from the route of the A9 from the south, as it descends Drumossie Moor down towards Inverness. Alternatively, an excellent elevated view may be obtained from the Black Isle itself, looking down to Fort George, Ardersier and Chanonry Ness from the Eathie road which runs along the high eastern side of the peninsula beyond Rosemarkie.

When this late surge of ice came to an end due to reduced falls of snow over the high ground, the snout of the glacier began to waste away and the ice front to retreat. The result was the deposition of a vast terminal moraine, formed from broken down rock gouged and plucked from the land in the glacier's powerful seaward progress.

In time, this huge morainic mass became broken and shaped by the sea into the peninsula now known as Chanonry Ness, and into the corresponding protrusion on which the defences of Fort George were constructed. Wind and weather may together have shaped the extremity of the Ness into something resembling a spit, but the abundant grey pebbles on the beach tell their own tale of the peninsula's more westerly glacial origins.

Elsewhere, the same metamorphic rock type provides a valuable clue to the source of the ice itself. Pieces of distinctive Inchbae augen gneiss, a rock which occurs only in one area about twenty-five miles away, have been identified in several Black Isle locations, proof positive of the westerly origins of the ice which once masked the peninsula.

One of the most obvious and interesting remnants of this glacial deposition dominates the village of Rosemarkie. The Red Craig which overlooks the settlement is a huge mass of glacial material whose reddish colouring clearly reflects its sandstone origins. Closer inspection of the deposit from the path which passes along its base suggests a degree of water sorting in its formation.

A short distance inland, the intriguing area known as The Dens has been designated a Site of Special Scientific Interest by virtue of its unusual character. The Dens consist of several deep ravines cut into the moraine by fast water flow, exposing the bare boulder-studded clays and gravels and creating a strangely raw landscape at odds with the leafy attraction of the Fairy Glen below.

For generations The Dens have been known for their earth pillars, features well known from Alpine valleys, but rare in this country. Where a particularly large boulder has been exposed by weathering and erosion of the moraine, it may act for some time as a sort of umbrella to the material below, shielding it from further erosion. As the sides of the pillar become worn, the feature becomes more accentuated, till at last the protective cap topples and the exposed pillar wastes away. Sometimes a capping of turf may serve the same purpose, acting as a temporary shield to the soft clay below.

The wild torrents of meltwater which flowed rapidly seawards as the ice wasted away were also to carve their own characteristic landforms. On the Cromarty Firth side, for example, between Jemimaville and Cromarty, a whole series of deep gulleys etch the land just above the road. Once again, local belief found a supernatural explanation for these features. It was not the gulleys which were considered interesting, though, but the intervening masses of morainic material, for they were believed to be the graves of giants.

The raw landscape of the Dens, looking across the firth to Ardersier. From time to time, strange-looking earth pillars form when the red clay underneath has been protected from weathering and erosion.

Between Avoch and Fortrose the engineers who laid down the Black Isle branch railway line met a real challenge in another set of deep ravines between the two villages.

Clearly, the vast quantities of water unlocked by the melting of the ice were bound to raise the sea level. The consequences for the Black Isle were to be far-reaching, for the land had been depressed by the weight of ice while it was resting on top. The result was a period of coastal erosion when the sea stood at a much higher level than it does today. In fact, it was actually at several different levels, the highest corresponding with the post-glacial maximum, and the others marking off successive rises of the land after its ice burden had been removed.

Where the sea was at its highest, caves were opened up in weak sections of cliff, and rock stacks resulted from marine erosion and coastal collapse. Today, these features stand high and dry above the level of even the wildest winter seas and storms. There are several examples beyond Rosemarkie, but the most spectacular is the fine natural arch at McFarquhar's Bed near Cromarty.

The fluctuating sea levels also produced a series of features that were to be of fundamental importance for village sites throughout the Black Isle. Where flat raised beaches occur, lines of housing invariably mark their presence. Charleston and North Kessock, Avoch, Fortrose, Rosemarkie and Cromarty – all reflect to varying degrees in their shape the presence of these raised beach features.

In this, the peninsula has similarities with many other coastal communities throughout northern Scotland, but in the patterns of its landscape the Black Isle has its own characteristics, a fact that has contributed to its distinctive regional personality.

CHAPTER 3

Wildlife of the Firthlands

Surrounded by the waters of the tidal firths, it is not surprising that the Black Isle is rich in wildlife interest. Indeed, some of these firthland areas are of significance not only in a local context, but nationally, and even internationally, for the rich wildlife habitats which they provide.

The innermost of these encircling water bodies is the Beauly Firth. Though really a landward extension of the sea, this tidal stretch above the Kessock narrows has a character of its own. At high tide, the firth is one unrelieved stretch of water, but low tide lays bare a vast spread of mud. The emptying Beauly River imparts to its firth the fertility of the land it has crossed. It is a process which has gone on since the waning of the ice-sheet, and the rich feeding in the deposits is a major attraction to wintering wildfowl.

In strength of numbers, greylag geese are the most important, their excited calls echoing across the winter firth as the V-shaped skeins arrive and depart from feeding forays into the surrounding farmlands. In the late 1950s, local birdwatchers first noted the presence of moulting Canada geese on the firth in summer. Numbers gradually increased until several hundred of these 'black' geese were making this moult migration. After some individuals were rounded up and marked with numbered leg rings, it was discovered that they originated in Yorkshire and adjacent areas. Somehow they had learned to make the journey north to moult their flight feathers in the peace and quiet of the Beauly Firth, and now the Canada goose flocks have become quite a summer wildlife attraction of the area.

Winter also brings in the ducks. In the short days, hundreds of wigeon graze the tidal flats, the drakes' wild whistling a characteristic sound of the season. Mallard and teal occur in significant numbers, but the saw-bill ducks are perhaps the most important feature of the winter firth. Of these, red-breasted mergansers occur in large groups, but it is the presence of hundreds of goosanders that puts the Beauly Firth on the European conservation map, for gatherings on such a scale are most uncommon. Viewed in good light, the goosander drakes are a beautiful sight with their iridescent green heads, suffused pink chests and bright red bills.

Although mute swans are the more numerous, Icelandic whooper swans, with their yellow and black patterned bills, are regular winter visitors. They like to gather near the upper firth where the river empties into the tidal flow, and small herds may often be seen grazing on nearby fields. The wild bugling of the whoopers is one of the most evocative sounds of the winter firthlands.

The mudflats also attract large wader flocks. Oystercatcher, redshank and lapwing are common, and all three species also nest locally. The haunting call of curlews carries across the mudflats in the clear air of winter days, and flocks of bar-tailed godwit, dunlin and knot all come to feed in the firth.

When the tide falls, it is always worth looking for the firth or common seals which haul up on to the sandbanks as they are laid bare by the outgoing water. As they relax in the security of these traditional resting places, they take on the shape of old-fashioned baby feeding bottles, their heads and tails upturned in a curve as their coats dry in the breeze.

Whales occasionally venture right up the firth. In 1883, a whale measuring forty-two feet in length was shot and brought ashore at Redcastle. Its carcase was eventually towed across to the canal basin at Inverness and loaded on to two rail trucks for transport south to Birmingham.

A few miles away, the spreads of eel grass in Munlochy Bay attract large numbers of wintering wildfowl, as do the seeds of saltwort which shares this tidal habitat. The wildfowl and wader flocks belong to the same population which haunts the Beauly Firth, and it is also a good place to see shelducks gathered on the fields in the springtime. Mute swans sometimes nest on the saltmarsh at the head of the bay, but in common with the other swans which make their seaweed nest mounds around the firths, they may lose their eggs during high tides.

There is a convenient stopping place provided with picnic tables above the bay on the Avoch road. This allows a good view across to the forested opposite slope and to the bare outline of Craigiehowe at the bay mouth. The Craigiehowe

Encircled by farmland, the muddy expanse of Udale Bay is of international importance as a nature reserve, attracting large flocks of wildfowl and waders.

slopes are the haunt of a flock of wild goats which may sometimes be spotted through binoculars as they browse among the bracken. These are the feral descendants of domesticated stock which took to the wild generations ago from some of the crofts where they were kept for their milk.

Winter is best for seeing the wildfowl flocks, though there are invariably a few summering geese which have been injured by gunshot during the winter and which have been unable to make the long spring flight northwards with the others. Even in summer, however, there is usually plenty of interest in the bay, such as roosting herons on the saltmarsh, mallard, teal and shelduck around the margins, and the odd sparrowhawk or buzzard out on a hunting foray from the nearby forests.

The small expanse of tidal flats at Avoch Bay provides some attraction as a feeding place for waders, while redshanks and shelducks sometimes feed on the mud inside the silted harbour. Mute swans gather in small numbers around the sewage outfall, and the pickings occasionally attract a pale-plumaged glaucous gull to add interest to the winter flock of herring and black-headed gulls.

21

The presence of vast flocks of scrounging herring gulls at the Longman rubbish tip in Inverness is almost certainly responsible for the current spread of roof nesting in the Black Isle seaside villages, a source of annoyance to residents who do not appreciate the gulls' over-enthusiastic contribution to the dawn chorus.

On the opposite side of the peninsula, a narrow area of mudflats runs parallel to the firth-side road between Cromarty and Jemimaville, allowing good glimpses of feeding waders when the tide is nearly full. But perhaps the most interesting site is the wide bay which faces across to industrial Invergordon on the opposite side of the firth.

This is Udale Bay, a vast spread of sand and mud deposits at low tide, and one half of a National Nature Reserve which includes also the Nigg Bay tidal flats on the opposite shore. In conservation terms, it is a highly significant area, and indeed has international importance in an age when bird populations are increasingly regarded as a concern transcending political boundaries. Indeed, the Nigg-Udale Bay area, and Cromarty Firth generally, together constitute one of the most important unspoiled estuarine sites left in the country.

There is an excellent car parking area on the side of the bay where the Newhall Burn enters the firth, just outside Jemimaville. From here, mallard, teal, goldeneye, shelduck and wigeon may all be seen in good numbers, the latter descending in their thousands from summering areas in Eastern Europe. Winter greylags present a magnificent sight as the skeins flight against the snowy outline of Ben Wyvis. Herons are common, as they are throughout the firths, and are often to be seen, hunch-backed and miserable-looking, at the head of the saltings.

Perhaps the most exciting wildlife spectacle of Udale Bay is the autumn gathering of waders and wildfowl which use the area as a staging post on their southerly migration routes. The mudflats act like a magnet to thousands of bird migrants. By early August, the first trickle of birds is passing southwards. By September and early October it is as if a northern floodgate has been opened, allowing countless birds to rush through.

Tight groups of grey knot swirl and twist above the tideline, catching the autumn light as they perform their split-second

Fulmar petrel, a characteristic bird of the summer cliffs. Fulmars make no nest, laying their single chalky white egg on bare ledges.

manoeuvres. Crowds of tiny dunlin rise and fall like the clouds of tundra insects they have left behind in Arctic wastes, and flocks of bar-tailed godwits chatter excitedly as they follow the ebb-tide, gathered in lines to probe their long bills into the ooze.

At high tide, the whole area is inundated by inflowing sea water, and all wader feeding is brought to a stop. Above high water mark, crowds of roosting birds gather to rest and preen. Heads tucked snugly into back feathers, they look deceptively relaxed, till the slightest danger signal puts them instantly into the air, wheeling and twisting as they disperse to some quieter place.

The occasional appearance of a wandering peregrine falcon among the winter bird flocks throws the whole bird scene into chaos. Alarmed by the sudden, menacing arrival of this spectre at their feast, the waders and wildfowl rise in crowded confusion. But there is safety in numbers, and such a streamlined hunter must at all costs avoid collision damage, preferring to pick out a singleton for the chase.

So far, the birds of Udale Bay have lived in comparative

harmony with industrial development across the water. Indeed, on one occasion, industrialisation acted to the dubious benefit of some birds. In the early days of the new grain distillery at Invergordon, wintering groups of gulls, ducks and swans soon discovered the effluent discharge and found themselves slightly intoxicated, and immortalised in local folksong as a result!

> *'In Invergordon by the sea*
> *They've built a new distillery,*
> *An' a' the gulls are on the spree*
> *That live in Invergordon.'*

It seems that moderation in all things was a dictum unknown to the birds which dined on the heady discharge of the distillery, and which were reputed to fly in a decidedly erratic manner afterwards!

On the whole, the wildlife interest of the Cromarty Firth is perhaps greater along its northern shore, but where the River Conon has deposited its load of silt there are small deltaic islands, ungrazed by farm animals and with a covering of alder and willow. Construction of the road bridge over the River Conon has given an opportunity for viewing the upper part of this fine natural site. Further downstream, it may be worthwhile looking for the firth seals which haul up on the mudflats on the seaward side of the Cromarty Firth bridge.

The varied physical form of the Black Isle cliffs is matched by their strong wildlife interest. Overlooking the sheltered arm of Munlochy Bay, the cliff edge of the Craigiehowe conglomerate outcrop is clothed in pines and other trees. The winter cormorant roost on Craigiehowe can be an extraordinary sight, when hundreds of these primitive-looking black birds leave their roosting trees and cliff ledges. Their silent seaward passage usually goes unnoticed as they flight low along the coast, but in the half light of a winter's afternoon they make an eerie, soundless sight against the last glow of sunset. In summer, the Craigiehowe cliffs resound to the cackling of fulmars in this most inland of their firth breeding sites.

At Fortrose, the cliffs beyond the harbour are covered in spreads of naturalised yellow tree lupins and blue periwinkle. Located nearby is a long-established colony of milk thistle with tall, spiky flower heads. This plant was once widely grown in the gardens of ecclesiastical establishments because, in religious folklore, the white veining on the leaves was held to represent the milk spilled from the breast of the Virgin Mary.

This is the only colony of this showy plant anywhere in the area, and it has been known at this site for a very long time. Perhaps its presence in a settlement with such a strong church history should cause no surprise, for it may represent a living link with the past. A few years ago, when a new drain was being laid under a street close to the Cathedral, some surplus soil was removed to another part of the village. Almost immediately, a large crop of milk thistle seedlings appeared, suggesting that the seeds are viable for a long time.

At Rosemarkie, the descendants of the noisy jackdaws which were certainly around the Red Craig cliff early last century are still a familiar part of the village scene today. In spring and summer they share their nesting places with the fulmars which first colonised the cliff in the early part of the present century, during an extraordinary, round-Britain expansion from their St Kilda power base. A few fulmars even venture inland among the bare red outcrops of the nearby Dens, in a strangely sylvan setting for such wanderers of the lonely ocean wastes.

Beyond Rosemarkie beach, the cliffs take on a different form. Since the time when they were last actively eroded thousands of years ago by high-level seas after the Ice Age, they have become heavily clothed in vegetation. In spring, carpets of wild hyacinths appear, a blue mist above clumps of pale yellow primroses, before the curled bracken fronds rise above them like living croziers. Early May sees the steep faces brightened by spreads of meadow saxifrage, like the clinging snow of an unseasonal blizzard. Later, the stunning red flowers of the bloody cranesbill enliven the steepest grassy slopes, while succulent English stonecrop clings to bare rock faces yellowed by lichen growth. Dyer's rocket, rock rose, lamb's lettuce, moonwort fern, wood vetch and hemp agrimony are also part of the varied botanical interest of this stretch of coastline.

Sunny days in early summer bring out the cliff-face butterflies, pearl-bordered fritillaries for the most part, but neatly marked small heaths are also common and the unpretentious dingy skipper sometimes puts in an appearance.

B

In places, the cliff face is smothered in spreading ivy out of which unseen wrens blast out their echoing song. Fulmar, jackdaw and rock dove all nest along cliffs in whose updraught raven and buzzard glide and wheel. The name Scart Craig locally applied to one section of cliff suggests that the cormorants or scarts have been using it as a roosting place for generations, covering the rock in an unsavoury whitewash.

Shelducks sometimes bring out a brood from a well-hidden nesting hole, perhaps in an old rabbit burrow, but the ducklings are invariably picked off by great black-backed gulls. These and herring gulls sometimes nest among the rock screes and along the shore. Such ground nesters are heavily predated by foxes which may sometimes be seen going about their business in broad daylight, annoyed by dive-bombing crows resentful of their presence. Roe deer often browse the cliff face vegetation, but their subtle colouring ensures that they usually pass unseen among the bracken and whins.

At Eathie, where the burn tumbles seawards through its deep den, just as it did in Hugh Miller's time, the present-day amateur geologist can stand and stare at the rock exposures from which the famous Cromarty geologist once extricated his fish fossils and pondered the Black Isle's geological past.

Sandy beaches are not well represented. There is one extensive area, however, stretching from Chanonry Point along to Rosemarkie and beyond. On the eastern flank of Chanonry Ness and just beyond Rosemarkie, are some hummocky areas suggesting old dune formations, now stabilised by vegetation. The former area is today the most testing part of the golf course, with its challenging humps and hollows rich in wild flowers such as meadow saxifrage, yellow rattle, harebell, eyebright and thyme over which blue butterflies flight on bright summer days.

A special feature of these areas is the cream-flowered burnet rose which delicately perfumes the still air of June evenings. Appropriately, it is also in these same places that the lovely six-spot burnet moth may be encountered, its red-spotted wings shining in green iridescence. Later, the shortening days of late summer bring the field gentian into a flowering carpet of pointed mauve blooms in this same type of habitat.

The upper beach is the place to look for the spreading mats

Harebell, commonly known as the Scots bluebell, is a common plant of the sandy seashore turf. Occasionally, the flowers are pure white instead of the normal pale blue.

of sea campion, topped by a profusion of papery white flowers. The fleshy sea purslane colonises the upper sandy beach, and high tides sometimes wash the sand away from its stringy roots. Sea rocket also inhabits the upper beach areas where its pale lilac flowers open cheerfully among the unsightly flotsam.

Skylarks nest plentifully on the golf course, their soaring song a feature of the area from earliest spring to summer as they flutter above well-concealed nest sites, unlike their meadow pipit cousins which descend in a parachute display. Rock pipits occur here and there along the shore, but in the winter time little groups of up to a dozen of these dark-plumaged birds may be seen feeding on the nearby fairways. Pied wagtails similarly like to hawk for insects on the golf course greens, especially in August and early September when large numbers gather. Oystercatchers also enjoy this man-made habitat, probing their strong red bills into the grass and helping to aerate the soil.

Stonechats used to be a feature of the whin bushes, noisily scolding the golfers on their search for errant balls, but a series of bad winters wiped them out and they have never recolonised the area. Gone, too, are the common terns. Their dive-bombing attacks used to be an unusual course hazard as their screaming mingled with the colourful expletives of irate golfers. Now the terns prefer instead the quieter beaches across the firth where a few little terns also make their nest scrapes. Luckily, however, these diminutive 'sea swallows' cross the firth to hawk and hunt along the tideline of the Black Isle. Their larger, noisier relations, the sandwich terns, fare no better where beaches are disturbed in summer, but some enterprising birds found a substitute nesting place among the bark chips in an empty log barge moored off Munlochy Bay.

Ringed plovers face the same disturbance problems, but a few birds attempt to take up a breeding territory each year. In recent times, one of the pairs of ringed plovers consisted of a perfectly normal bird and another which was leucistic, that is to say its body colouring was so dilute that from a distance it looked white.

Autumn migration brings many waders to Chanonry Point. Amongst the earliest are turnstones in their russet tortoiseshell plumage, but this soon fades to an undistinguished pattern of winter grey and white. Sanderlings, tiny grey waders from the north, sometimes trickle through in small numbers, but the dunlin flocks are a more obvious feature of the winter months, and they are sometimes joined by a few knot and bar-tailed godwits.

Lapwings begin to gather into a large flock on Chanonry Ness in July. August brings a small passage of whimbrel, smaller northern relations of the curlew, but it is usually only their repetitive overhead calling that draws attention to their presence. Golden plover occasionally pass through, and on one recent autumn evening a confiding dotterel paused briefly on one of the golf course fairways on its way from some high mountain top to its wintering place in the sunny south.

Short-eared owls sometimes visit the golf course in winter, quartering the rough grass areas in broad daylight in search of voles. Even buzzards are sometimes drawn to hunt among the abundant seaside rabbits when snow has blanketed the area round about.

At the extremity of this peninsula within a peninsula,

Salmon fishers at Rosemarkie. Fishing with net and coble has been a feature of the firths for many generations.

Chanonry Point has a reputation as a place for observing birds passing through the narrows. Fortunately, in this exposed place, there is a good parking area from which the incomings and outgoings may easily be observed.

Manx shearwaters are frequent wanderers from the open sea, but the darker sooty shearwater occurs only rarely. The tiny Leach's petrel has been seen near the lighthouse, and on one occasion, the lightkeeper recovered a storm petrel from an outhouse, the bird having entered, appropriately enough, through a pop-hole provided for the lighthouse hens.

The piratical skuas are regular autumn visitors. One of the best clues to their presence is the screaming of terns being harried for the fish which they have caught. Arctic skuas in their different colour phases, pass through in considerable numbers. The bulky great skuas or bonxies are also regular visitors, and the much rarer pomarines have been surprisingly frequent in recent years, some even lingering throughout the winter. Sometimes they fly low past the lighthouse as fierce autumn squalls drive them into the Inner Firth, and it is then that the curiously twisted tail feathers of the pomarines may be seen. Much scarcer on autumn passage are long-tailed skuas, but on one occasion an individual sat out an equinoctial gale on the golf course.

Scores of red-throated divers perform a winter feeding movement into the firth in the early mornings, and a reverse roosting flight out to the open sea as the light fails. Sometimes these divers call out the strange and eerie call of the rain goose of northern mythology as they flight in from their night-time roost. Black-throated divers are much scarcer, and great northern divers venture through the narrows only rarely.

Guillemots gather in the firth in huge winter numbers when fish stocks are high, while razorbills maintain a lesser presence, and puffins are quite uncommon. Little auks are rare winter visitors from their high latitude breeding places, but at the end of 1987, an unprecedented arrival brought several hundreds of these tiny black and white seabirds to the Point.

Slavonian grebes, in autumn a pale shadow of their superb summer breeding plumage of russet body feathering and golden ear tufts, sometimes venture down to the firth from nesting haunts on nearby upland lochs. A few Canada geese on their summer moult migration may stop off to drink and preen at the mouth of the Rosemarkie Burn, while brent geese are rare winter visitors.

There is always a good chance of seeing the whiskered snout of a common or a grey seal as it surveys the scene beside the lighthouse, and this is probably the best place anywhere along the Moray Firth to see bottle-nosed dolphins breaking the surface or leaping clean out of the water in their impressive displays. Sadly, these lovely animals are now in decline around our shores, but, for the moment at least, the dolphins which frequent the waters around the Black Isle can still delight visitors with their breathtaking antics.

But if there is one sound and sight which encapsulates the very spirit of winter days in these northern firthlands, it is the ringing calls and mad flighting displays of long-tailed ducks. 'Coal an' can'le licht' is how East-coast folk used to translate this wild calling into human speech. Occasionally, the long-tails venture close enough to shore for the drakes' jaunty tail feathers and winter plumage of soft grey, brown and cream to be clearly seen. But, as often as not, these fascinating birds conduct this animated display far from human gaze, their wild calls echoing through the darkening and frosty air of a Black Isle winter evening.

CHAPTER 4
Woodland Wildlife

Woodland and forest make a significant contribution to the Black Isle scene. They punctuate the farmlands and are an important element of the patchwork landscape so much appreciated by both visitor and resident. While it is true to say that few, it any, truly natural woodland areas now remain, there are patches of semi-natural tree cover here and there to complement the formal forestry plantations.

Unfortunately, the value of some of these fragments has not always been appreciated, and many seem fated to disappear as a result. This is particularly so with the small stands of birchwood. Some are regarded by farmers as useful areas of winter shelter for cattle, and the inevitable consequence is that natural regeneration of the woodlands does not take place, for

The way things used to be – unimproved land near Whitebog. A few patches of juniper-dominated heathland have escaped the efforts of the farming improvers. They make an interesting addition to a landscape dominated by farmland and forest.

the cattle trample or graze any potential replacement tree seedlings. Others are under pressure from the realisation of their potential as building sites. A small wood is an attractive setting for a house, but the long term future of such areas looks bleak.

Broad-leaved woodland has a key role both as a wildlife habitat and in providing a visual amenity. The character of the autumn countryside is derived as much from the colouring of the deciduous trees as from the yellow of the harvest fields. Even in winter, the pale bark and reddish branches of birch provide an attractive combination at an otherwise dead time of year, while in spring the opening of the new birch leaves spreads through the woodlands like a delicate green haze. The summer song of the willow warbler is probably heard most often in birch woods, and a variety of small birds such as coal, blue, great and long-tailed tits, tree creepers, chaffinches, siskins and redpolls are attracted to feed in them.

Juniper also faces an uncertain future in the Black Isle. Originally, this attractive evergreen shrub would have occurred in an open woodland situation, with mature bushes attaining a considerable height. Now, juniper bushes in any quantity survive only in a few areas of land which have resisted past attempts at improvement, and which tend now to be regarded only as 'scrub' grazing. As a result, most surviving junipers (such as those which may be seen along the main Cromarty road beyond Rosemarkie) are old and gnarled, and there is a dearth of regeneration.

The disappearance of the juniper would be a real loss from the Black Isle countryside, for it was part of the old Caledonian Forest which once dominated the northern countryside. It is an attractive plant in its own right, with bluish-green foliage and dark berries which carry a misty bloom as they ripen. When crushed they give off the distinctive smell of gin, for it is these same berries which are used to impart the characteristic flavour to the spirit.

Small, but significant, stands of deciduous trees are scattered throughout the peninsula. The attractive Craig Woods which clothe the old fossil cliff between Avoch and Fortrose not only protect the busy road below from soil slumping, but provide a fine backcloth to the coast route. For the most part, they consist of tall mature beeches with smooth grey trunks, and of gnarled old oaks, with ferns sprouting from their mossy branches.

In fact, the present Craig Wood seems to have replaced an earlier one sacrificed for the nation's strategic needs. Concerned at the prospect of invasion by sea during the eighteenth century, the authorities ordered that massive quantities of wood be brought in to Fort George to form protecting pallisades, and, of course, the Black Isle was well placed to supply this need.

In the autumn, the broad-leaved woodlands provide a splendid sight in their rich end-of-season colouring. Nowhere is this more evident than in the mixed hardwood plantings of the old policy woodlands, such as those around the big houses of Rosehaugh (now demolished), Braelangwell and Newhall. The oakwood at Drummondreach on the Cromarty Firth side is a survival of semi-natural deciduous woodland of considerable age. Once, its oak bark was in demand locally as a source of tanning material, but now this small surviving woodland is left undisturbed.

The deciduous woodlands often have a rich botanical interest. Wild hyacinth, wood sorrel, wood anemone, violet, woodrush and primrose form the woodland carpet, while honeysuckle wraps itself tightly around tree trunks as it reaches towards the light. The lax yellow and white honeysuckle flowers are a pale shadow of the richly coloured cottage garden varieties, but they have a sweet perfume that permeates the early summer woods when the wild hyacinths carpet the woodland floor in a rich shade of blue.

Wild garlic imparts its less delicate perfume to the woodland air, its starry white May flowers followed by rapid yellowing and die-back of broad green leaves. Wood sanicle, an unpretentious pinkish-white flower of great charm, is another resident of these areas.

One of the most fascinating of all woodland plants occurs where shady situations seem to suit it best. The tiny moschatel might very easily be overlooked, for it blends easily into the background. It is sometimes known as town hall clock, since its greenish flowers are set in a curious arrangement on four sides of a square. The very scarce and strange-looking coral-root orchid survives in a mixed woodland area of the Black Isle where it has been known from the early part of this century. It belongs to a group of orchids which depend on a fungal growth at their roots to absorb plant foods from the humus in which the coral-like root system spreads. The odd, greenish flowers may easily be missed, and the coral-root adds to its mysterious ways by not appearing at all some years, but lying low until enough food has been stored up to support another flowering.

The even rarer bird's nest orchid is a strange, honey-coloured flowering plant which shares the same unusual subterranean existence as the coral-root. It occurs at only one woodland site in the Black Isle, and this shady corner is one of its furthest north flowering localities in the British Isles.

The open character of the deciduous woodlands is appreciated by insects as well as plants. The speckled wood butterfly, though common further south, is localised in the eastern Highlands. It evidently finds the Black Isle to its taste, however, for it can be seen on the wing in early summer days. At rest, it quickly merges into the background, its speckled wings blending perfectly into the pattern of dappled woodland light.

Scattered all over the countryside are little groups of old pines. Their existence points to a more extensive covering by these trees in the past. A specially interesting, indeed unique, area is the Monadh Mor, near Tore, a highly rated Site of Special Scientific Interest. Its significance, in conservation terms, lies in the fact that it is the best surviving fragment in the whole of Britain of forest bog with Boreal affinities, meaning that it represents the nearest thing to a scene more typical of the Scandinavian northlands.

The whole Monadh Mor area has defied attempts at drainage and reclamation in the past, and now has the appearance of a confused mixture of Scots pine, bog land and intervening acid ponds. In fact, there is a pattern to the area, though perhaps not a very obvious one from ground level. The pines actually grow along fairly low ridges of glacial moraine, and the bogs lie in ill-drained intervening channels.

Following on from the creation of the Forestry Commission, a new generation of pine forest was established in the 1920s along the Mulbuie Ridge. Some landowners had already planted pine trees on this highest part of the peninsula early last century, though in the old accounts they are referred to as 'Scots firs', the old northern name for pines.

Some of these surviving early estate plantings of pine have now taken on an appearance reminiscent of old natural pine woods, with such typical understorey plants as blaeberry, starry white chickweed wintergreen, pale yellow cow wheat and rich yellow tormentil. The attractive, pale woodland orchid, creeping lady's tresses, also graces the floor of such places. Despite its name, the common wintergreen is really a rare plant within the Black Isle, but in the few places where it does occur it puts up tiered stems of white summer flowers reminiscent of lily-of-the-valley blooms.

In one of these old pine plantings on a memorable May morning, crested tit, redstart, crossbill and great spotted woodpecker all put in an appearance for the writer in the same small area, strongly recalling the atmosphere of the old Caledonian pine forest which now has its stronghold in the Spey valley.

Other conifer species have been established by the Forestry Commission, especially Sitka spruce and larch. Along some roadsides, notably across the elevated ridge at Mount High, berry-bearing cotoneaster and stranvesia shrubs were planted to add some colour and diversity to the edge of the plantations. In winter, the stranvesia is draped in huge berry clusters, though the birds evidently prefer the cotoneaster, leaving the spectacular stranvesia fruits for the enjoyment of passing motorists.

Autumn brings a new growth out of the previous year's decay. Fungi in almost countless variety grace the woodland floor where they rise and decay unseen. Sometimes, however, their appearance is quite eye-catching, as with the fly agaric, that white-spotted red toadstool so beloved of children's book illustrators.

There is little doubt that the old pine stands provide the most interest among the forestry plantations. Male crossbills are a splendid sight in spring, when they don their rich red breeding plumage. Loud ringing calls above the tree tops are invariably the best guide to their presence, but crossbills are most often seen in overhead silhouette. Through binoculars,

View towards Learnie Hill. The attractive patchwork of farmland and forest lends great attraction to the countryside, offering a variety of wildlife habitat.

this may allow an opportunity to see the curious cross mandibles which give the bird its name, and enable it to prise out seeds from tough pine cones.

Crested tits may have existed in the area in earlier times, but have now found a permanent niche in the Black Isle as a result of the extensive planting of Scots pine along the Mulbuie Ridge. This typically Scottish bird, emblem of the Scottish Ornithologists' Club, thrives in mature old pine forest with plenty of nesting sites in decaying and dead trees. The crested tit's opportunities for finding nesting sites in the well-managed Black Isle forest stands are considerably more limited.

Like crested tit and great spotted woodpecker, the capercaillie was also a typical bird of the old native pinewoods. In 1578, Bishop Leslie (sometime bishop in the Chanonry of Ross at Fortrose) wrote: 'In Rosse and Loquhaber, and utheris places amang hilis and knowis, ar nocht in missing fir trie sufficient, quhair oft sittis a certane fowl and verie rare called the Capercalye to name, with the vulgar peple, the horse of the forrest . . .'

37

Unlike the crested tit and great spotted woodpecker, the capercaillie succumbed completely to the pressure of forest clearance, and by the latter part of the eighteenth century was completely extinct as a native breeding bird. In time, however, this largest of all native game birds was to be reintroduced to the Highlands. The Black Isle capercaillies are therefore descended from those birds brought in from Scandinavia in the early part of last century and liberated in Perthshire to form the nucleus of a replacement stock.

For a time, there was a very healthy capercaillie population in the Black Isle forests, and birds could often be met with along fire-breaks and on the edges of plantations, but in recent years they have become quite scarce. This may be due to extensive predation by foxes, since the capercaillie is a ground nester, and hens and chicks are then vulnerable to attack.

A close encounter with a male capercaillie in the heart of the forest can be a heart-stopping affair, as the huge black bulk suddenly crashes upwards through the branches. At such moments, it is easy to see why folk called it the 'horse of the forests' in the old days. It would indeed be a sad loss if this impressive woodland bird was to disappear completely from the Black Isle scene.

Apart from the ubiquitous coal tit and other members of its family, one of the most distinctive of small bird species in the forestry plantations is the siskin. The little male in smart green and black plumage is a striking sight in the breeding season, but these are sociable birds and are rarely seen alone. During the winter, many siskins forage well away from their forest breeding places, visiting village gardens to feed from suspended bags of peanuts, a habit which has become widespread in recent years.

The sparrowhawk also ventures from the forests in the direction of the villages at the back-end of the year. Winter bird-tables are sometimes visited by sparrowhawks in search of easy pickings. It is not, however, the scraps on the table which form the attraction, but the concentration of small birds feeding on them. The sudden appearance of a sparrowhawk at a crowded bird-table is a memorable experience, as panic-stricken birds scatter in all directions.

Sparrowhawks have now regained the ground lost during

earlier decades when pesticides posed a threat to their continued survival. The scattered feathers of wood pigeons encountered along forest edges are a good indication of the importance of this other woodland dweller as a prey species. In late summer and autumn, young and inexperienced sparrowhawks sometimes kill themselves by flying into windows, perhaps while attempting to dash through an apparent gap as they would do in the confined spaces of a forestry plantation.

Tawny owls are nocturnal feeders, with the result that their presence usually goes unobserved. The amorous hooting from the woodlands confirms their occurrence wherever suitable nesting areas occur.

Buzzards breed in good numbers throughout the area. Although they require trees in which to construct their large twiggy nests, buzzards also need plenty of open space for hunting ground prey. The Black Isle combination of forest and open farmland is thus an ideal one. The sight of a buzzard sitting atop a telegraph pole or fence-post has become one of the most characteristic of countryside scenes, and one much appreciated by visitors from areas where this beautiful bird of prey is in short supply.

The buzzard's strong population is probably closely linked to the large concentrations of rabbits which may be seen grazing along woodland margins or scampering off the road at the approach of a car. Indeed, road casualties sometimes provide an early morning buzzard meal, but such carrion is more commonly removed by nature's efficient undertakers, the carrion crows.

On the whole, Black Isle crows are a mongrel lot, for they occur in the transition zone between the black crows of the south and grey-black hoodies typical of the north and west. Although they may look quite different, the two crows are really geographical forms of the same species, and interbreed quite freely. In fact, many Black Isle hoodies are nothing like as pure in plumage as the birds seen in the upland west, and after the breeding season some very ill-assorted family groups may be seen.

Although crows are never slow to exploit an opportunity to feast on a dead sheep or lamb, they were more regarded as vermin in the days when free-range poultry-keeping was prevalent, and game management more intensive. As a result of reduced persecution, they are probably more widespread than in the past, and their single tree nests are revealed throughout the countryside when winter removes the leaves from the branches.

Without doubt, crows are amongst the greatest opportunists of the bird world, and many have learned to exploit the possibilities for feeding in the villages. Cardboard cartons and foil-top bottles are dealt with in a few well-aimed blows from the bill of wily individuals which seek out unprotected milk deliveries.

By contrast, woodland rookeries are places of concentrated nesting activity, for rooks are much more sociable birds than their scavenging relations. In winter time, the Black Isle rooks regularly flight out from their roosts, crossing the Chanonry narrows to feed across the firth. Late afternoon sees them punching their way back into the wind or flying low across the wave-tops, usually in the noisy company of jackdaws. The latter are widespread throughout the Black Isle, but prefer their own nesting sites along the cliffs or in the dark recesses of chimney pots.

The reduction in persecution of so-called 'vermin' is almost certainly the reason for the recent increase in the other resident member of the crow family. Even in the mid 1970s there was hardly a magpie to be seen throughout the Black Isle, but in the last few years pairs of these distinctive pied birds have established themselves in many areas, once again where woodland and farmland are intermixed, providing an ideal combination of breeding and feeding opportunities.

On the wider Highland plane, fox, wild cat and pine marten have all considerably increased their numbers and distribution. Foxes are now common everywhere in the Black Isle, and some farmers complain of their great increase since forestry became widespread. It is not unusual now to see foxes in broad daylight, but they prefer to hunt when darkness gives them more cover.

In recent times, both wild cat and pine marten have become established in the Black Isle, though few people have come into contact with them. Unfortunately, ignorance still prevails, and

Beloved of illustrators of children's books, the fly agaric is a widespread fungus. The white-spotted red toadstools appear at the end of summer. Though poisonous to man, they are often nibbled by rodents.

in the past few years a number of wild cats have been shot.

The pine marten has, for many years, been spreading out of its stronghold in the North-west Highlands. Increasing tree cover has encouraged expansion of its range, and its recent presence in the Black Isle is related to this trend. With few free-range hens being kept about the farmyards these days, it is perhaps unlikely that the pine marten will come much into conflict with man, and it is to be hoped that the presence of this attractive mammal will be appreciated.

The red squirrel is one of the marten's prey species. It is reasonably common in the Black Isle conifer plantations, and fortunately, the alien grey squirrel, has not yet made inroads this far north. At ground level, stoats are often met with in the countryside, but nature sometimes plays a trick on them by changing them into ermine white in winters where there is no snow to hide them.

Roe deer exist in good numbers wherever there is suitable woodland habitat, and a morning or evening walk along a forest ride will usually reveal one or two feeding deer along the grassy strip. Surrounding farmlands are also visited, and roe deer may then be seen browsing in fields close to the forest edge. Earlier this century, Japanese Sika deer were introduced to the policies of Rosehaugh House by the proprietor. Although sika continue to thrive in other parts of Ross-shire, there is no sign of them having survived in the Black Isle.

In terms of their contribution to the diversity of the countryside, and as a habitat for plant and wildlife, the Black Isle woodlands and forests have an important role to play. The time has surely come, however, to arrest the decline of the smaller areas of broad-leaved woodland before they disappear for ever, taking all their natural interest with them. But their value does need to be recognised. To view them merely as 'scrub' land, fit only for removal or building development, is seriously to undervalue them both as wildlife habitats and as an essential part of the Black Isle countryside patchwork.

CHAPTER 5

The Living Farmlands

Like a tidal wave of change, the agricultural improvements of the eighteenth and nineteenth centuries spread across the face of the Black Isle countryside. Previously unmanaged wetland and moorland areas were engulfed and added to the existing farmland acres. Yet, despite such pressures, wildlife still adds an important living dimension to the Black Isle's farming countryside, either by having adapted to the process of change, or by surviving in the remnants of the old countryside which persist.

In the new farming order there was little place for what the improvers perceived to be 'waste' ground, and in the process of reclamation there were bound to be wildlife losses. The coveys of red grouse, for example, which once haunted the heathery Mulbuie Common were doomed to disappear along with their moorland habitat, since their lifestyle depended on the heather

Though farming transformed the face of the land, there is still plenty of variety in the Black Isle countryside.

43

shoots for food. The *Ross-shire Journal* noted on the 12th of August 1880 that nine brace of grouse had been bagged on the Rosehaugh portion of the moor, but that 'drainage had rendered the broods small'.

It must have been the same story for birds like the curlew which like to breed in damp places. Curlews are now uncommon Black Isle nesters, though they occur widely along the coast in winter and venture on to surrounding fields to probe their long curving bills into the farmland soils.

But if drainage and reclamation were to be responsible for the demise of nesting grouse and curlews, it was the increase in mechanisation that was to deal a blow to the once familiar lapwing. In the days when farmers walked behind a pair of horse, they would note the distress calls of the agitated birds and mark the position of their nesting scrapes. Many a clutch of well-camouflaged lapwing eggs was carefully removed in a ploughman's bonnet to be relocated in a safer place close by. But now, the evocative nesting cries of the lapwing are much scarcer sounds in the Black Isle spring air, and the countryside is the poorer for their passing. The corncrake has also vanished, along with the old hay and corn rigs, but its monotonous night-time 'crek-crek' calling is recalled with nostalgia by older country folk.

Recently gone, too, is the corn bunting which blurted out its pent-up song from roadside wires. As with the corncrake, some subtle variation in climatic environment may have helped the corn bunting on its way to local extinction, but undoubtedly the changes in the farming landscape have hastened its demise. The same cannot be said of its more showy bunting relation, the yellow-hammer, which must be a strong contender for the title of the Black Isle's most characteristic bird. This beautiful bird is closely associated with the roadside whins, and the sight of a singing male shouting his defiant 'Deil, deil, tak ye-ee!' song at a rival from the top of a bright yellow whin bush is surely one of the Black Isle's loveliest countryside features. (It should be noted that only English yellow-hammers sing 'A little bit of bread and no chee-eese!)

The reed bunting, with his smart black cap and white collar, is a much rarer sight, since the areas of bog land which this species prefers are now few and far between. The same habitat preference also limits the distribution of the skulking sedge warbler with its grating summer song, and even in recent years some of the last remnants of suitable rushy habitat for this bird have been lost through drainage and tree planting.

To some extent, the oystercatcher has replaced the lapwing as harbinger of spring on the farmlands. Once a purely coastal nester, the smartly plumaged black and white oystercatcher has long since moved inland to nest and rear its young. Indeed, some farmers take the same benign interest in these birds as they did in the lapwings in the old days, a fact much to the advantage of one Black Isle nesting pair. Following the recent fashion of the species elsewhere, a pair of oystercatchers decided one year to make their nest in the rotten top of a fence strainer post in Avoch parish. This unconventional site was well removed from the undesirable attention of stoat or fox, but did have the disadvantage of being right beside a busy road.

Nevertheless, the oystercatchers were successful in their elevated nesting place. When the rotting post was eventually replaced by a new one, it seemed that the birds had lost their desirable residence, but the nearby farmer nailed a hollowed-out piece of wood to the new post top. Obviously appreciative of this effort, the oystercatchers took to their replacement nest site with enthusiasm.

For some years, oystercatchers found a suitable substitute for a pebble beach on the flat roof of Fortrose Academy. Over several seasons, a nesting scrape was made among the small stones which cover the bitumen roof surface, and young were successfully hatched. The parent birds brought in a succession of long wriggling worms from the nearby fields, much to the interest of school pupils absorbed by this real-life biology lesson. Things were not to work out for the enterprising waders, however. Safe though their lofty nesting site was from the attention of prowling ground predators, it was highly accessible to nearby roof-nesting herring gulls which killed and removed the oystercatcher chicks to satisfy the appetite of their own hungry broods.

In the making of the Black Isle farmlands it was not only the birds that were to suffer from loss of habitat. Moorland and wetland plants were also destined to disappear, or at least to survive only in those remnants of habitat which remained. The most serious casualty on the plant list, since it involved a complete British extinction, was undoubtedly the alpine butterwort. Like its familiar blue-flowered relation, this extremely rare bog plant was an insect-eater, augmenting its meagre diet by absorbing nutrients from the bodies of its victims. The plant's fatal allure was its fleshy leaves which gave it the typical butterwort appearance of something resembling a sticky green starfish.

The alpine butterwort's delightful blooms were pale with a canary-yellow throat. In the whole of the British Isles its early summer flowering was to be seen only in the Black Isle, and even there exclusively in bogland in the hinterland of Avoch. Though always collectable by virtue of its extremely local distribution, the alpine butterwort fell victim to agricultural change. As its boggy home was drained and pressed into farming use, areas of suitable habitat became even more scarce.

Inevitably, increasing rarity only served to speed its end. Botanists were drawn to the Black Isle from all over the land, for the late nineteenth century was the age of the collecting box and the pressed flower collection. The result was that the peninsula's rarest flower totally vanished from the face of the land, but there is no shortage of faded herbarium specimens up and down the country.

Wherever drainage schemes posed greater difficulty, fragments of the old bog land were spared the drain and plough, at least until improved methods of tackling them could be developed. Those that have escaped the further onslaught of late twentieth century reclamation schemes remain as a fascinating reminder of the living landscape that has gone. The common butterwort still exudes its fatal sticky charms and enlivens the month of June with its elegant blue flowers, and sometimes shares its damp habitat with its fellow insectivore, the diminutive sundew.

Other flowering attractions of these remnant wetland places are the several members of the orchis family. Purple marsh orchids rise dramatically from a green backcloth of damp pasture in June. Tiny, pink-flowered fragrant orchids scent the still summer evenings, and greenish-white butterfly orchids maintain a precarious toe-hold in a few damp places. The lesser twayblade is an unusual member of the orchis family

The insect-eating butterwort survives in remaining wetland areas. Its rare cousin, the Alpine butterwort, was the victim of drainage and over-zealous nineteenth century botanists.

whose name is a reference to its twin-leaved character, and it also is confined to a very few remaining sites.

The yellow butterball globeflower, so attractive a feature of wet northern moors, finds a last refuge here and there on the Black Isle. But rarity is no guarantee of protection, however beautiful or interesting, and within the last few years one of the last surviving globe-flower colonies has been drained out of existence. The removal of such a delightful plant along with its fragment of wetland habitat merely to add to a mounting European farm surplus seemed an unjustifiable act.

Wherever small patches of undrained land still remain, the characteristic plants of the wetlands live on. Early summer brings the bright flowering of ragged robin, its frayed pink petals in untidy contrast to the rounded blooms of its commoner campion cousins. At a more lowly level, the diminutive ivy-leaved crowfoot sprawls across muddy hollows, putting out tiny white flowers as it goes. Late summer brings out the delicately veined white blooms of the Grass of Parnassus, a lovely flower now confined to a last few damp places.

In the kettle hole depressions around Muir of Ord, flag iris beds send up their flower spikes in early summer. Marsh cinquefoil, with its strange-looking dark purple flowers, inhabits the wettest places where a few mallard ducks and coots nest. Where the water level is highest, yellow buttercup flowers of spearwort rise above blue forget-me-nots around the edges of ponds, and the uncommon celery-leaved buttercup grows from favoured ditch-sides.

Old-established farmland and roadside ditches provide their own interest as oases of variety among flowerless fields. Where conditions are most to its liking, meadowsweet flourishes in fragrant lines, generously releasing its heady perfume into the summer air. Spectacular yellow flowerings of mimulus mark the lines of some farmland ditches. Though not a native plant, the mimulus has spread widely throughout the British countryside, evidently finding local conditions a suitable substitute for those of its North American homeland.

Apart from little Loch Lundie, hemmed in between two conglomerate ridges near Kessock, and the largely infilled Culbokie Loch, there are now no sizeable water bodies. Loch Scadden on the Rosehaugh estate had already been drained by the middle of last century. Wetland habitats of any size are now rare throughout the Black Isle, and there has been an unfortunate ongoing tendency to regard the surviving patches which remain as a challenge for further drainage, thereby robbing the countryside even more of its diversity and interest.

The so-called 'weeds of cultivation', whose summer blooming once brightened the country scene have also been forced into submission, this time by years of spraying and intensive land management. But in the no-man's land of the roadside verge, rich flowerings of campion in shades of red, pink and white enliven summer days, and provide enjoyment to passing road users.

Although so many wild flowers have retreated in the face of farming improvement, nature appears to have an infinite capacity for recovery when the opportunity arises, so that disturbed verges around road works quickly sport a covering of cheery-faced purple heartsease pansies, of showy red poppies, or of yellow corn marigolds. Wherever a concentrated summer flowering of annuals has occurred, winter flocks of finches eagerly seek out the withered remains and spend weeks sifting methodically through dead seed heads. Large flocks of chaffinches and greenfinches are often joined by bramblings down from the north, the rich russet plumage of the males a striking sight as they search for seeds scattered on the ground.

Sometimes a few goldfinches join these winter weed feasts, their musical twittering as much a clue to their presence as their bright red heads and golden yellow wing-bars. These beautiful birds have increased markedly in the Black Isle in recent years. They are more specialised feeders than the larger finches, and seem most at home on seeding thistle heads, sending the thistledown flying on the breeze as they prise out tiny seeds. Snowy winters bring groups of yellow-hammers together, often foraging with the finches in flocks several hundred strong. And when the weather is at its very worst, a few reed buntings and even some snow buntings may join the gatherings.

The pale lilac flowers of lady's smock, once widespread in damp places, line damp Black Isle roadsides, appearing in May and lasting into June. They owe their survival to the wet conditions found in and around the roadside ditches, and their continued presence is of importance to one of the Black Isle's most beautiful insects. The orange-tip butterfly is here at the northern end of its range. Only the male has the bright orange tips to its white wings. This gives it a kind of twinkling flight which the female lacks as she inspects the ditch sides during her brief flying season, pausing every so often to survey a suitable looking plant on which she might deposit her clutch of eggs. Small tortoiseshell butterflies are sometimes abundant on sunny summer days. They thrive wherever patches of nettles and thistles have been left to flourish and flower along the no-man's land that is the roadside verge.

Black Isle verges vary in their botanical interest according to many factors. Those close to old established woods often allow the woodland flora to creep out towards the edge of the road. Primrose, common violet, wood sorrel, wood anemone and chickweed wintergreen all occur in this way. Drier verges occasionally favour the occurrence of rest harrow with its pink and white summer pea flowers, while moister conditions are to the liking of the colonial butterbur. At the very beginning of the year, the prominent white butterbur flowers unfurl out of fat bursting buds which have pushed through the cold ground. Later in the season, the huge rhubarb-like leaves uncurl, completely blanketing the banks where they grow. The vast spreads of early butterbur flowers provide a particular attraction along the burnside at Newhall, close by the road.

In shadier places, the white umbrella heads of myrrh or sweet cicely open above feathery green foliage that smells deliciously of aniseed on a warm early summer's day. The related, but much taller, alien giant hogweed is of limited occurrence, but does grow along a few roadside verges.

In the old days of farming, the Black Isle countryside would have been ablaze with the colours of the flowering field annuals. Intensive husbandry has now severely limited their range, but during recent years, the cornflower, one of the most typical of all the old farmland flowers, has shown signs of a come-back. Along the edge of cereal fields in Killearnan parish, cornflowers have again enlivened the country scene and helped recall the flowering glory of a bygone farming age. Where they occur, the bright blue flowers stand out in showy contrast to the sombre yellow of the ripening barley stalks through which they twine.

But of the cornflower's one-time companion plant in the old time fields, the corn cockle, there is now no trace. In the early nineteenth century, one writer could note that this reddish-purple flower of the old farmlands was 'too common' in Ross-shire, but those were the days before chemical sprays and more intensive farming methods were to rob the Black Isle countryside of so much of its botanical colour. One of the greatest delights of the Black Isle farming landscape, much remarked upon by visitors, is the blaze of flowering whins which brightens the country scene in May and June. Grazing damage by rabbits, which find a refuge under its prickly canopy, and the trend towards larger fields have both encouraged farmers to remove bordering lines of this spectacular prickly shrub. Yet, despite the onslaught, vast quantities of whins still remain to scent the warm air of early summer days, and to provide valuable cover for linnets and yellow-hammers.

An interesting feature of whin bushes is that they are often heavily grazed in their younger stages by rabbits, resulting in

The small tortoiseshell is one of the commonest Black Isle butterflies. This attractive insect thrives wherever its food plants have escaped the onslaught of farmland 'improvement.'

what looks like green pincushion mounds on the ground. Most of the older bushes are out of reach of rabbit grazing, but when they are in flower, a distinct browse line can be seen, marking the highest point which an adult rabbit can reach when standing on its hind legs.

In the old days, the cultivated fields could offer a nesting habitat for a variety of birds. Now, few species can successfully fit their nesting requirements into the management pattern of today's farmlands. Perhaps the best example of adaptation in the farming areas is provided by the swallow. Few farms are without at least one pair of these cheery summer visitors, flying in and out of barns and outhouses and hawking over the surrounding fields, just as they did in farming days gone by. Some are a bit more adventurous, seeking out a nesting place in village outhouses and garages. But the grandest nesting site by far is up in the vaulted roof of the remaining part of Fortrose Cathedral where a pair of swallows sometimes set up home. As visitors stop to admire the cathedral's fine stonework, the unconcerned swallows swoop in and out of the arched windows, recalling Shakespeare's 'guest of summer, the temple-haunting martlet' in 'Macbeth'.

Among the so-called 'game' birds, partridges have undergone a decline in numbers, though small winter coveys show themselves at roadsides. Pheasants are locally very plentiful, for example in farmland around the policies of Rosehaugh, where stocks are kept at a high level for shooting purposes. Brightly plumaged cock pheasants may often be seen before dusk, foraging around the edges of fields, but the more highly camouflaged females are less noticed. Hares are also shot during game shoots, though their numbers have undergone a decline in recent times.

The Black Isle farmlands provide a focus of feeding activity for vast numbers of wood pigeons. Winter flocks, sometimes several hundreds of birds strong, descend to feed on crops, causing farmers to resent the availability of so many suitable roosting places in the surrounding forestry plantations. The wood pigeon's smaller relation, the collared dove, colonised the Black Isle at a fairly early stage after its initial move into Britain. After a rapid spread from Eastern Europe in the 1950s, the first Scottish nesting took place at Covesea across the Moray Firth. Now autumn and winter gatherings of fifty or more birds may be seen lining telephone wires around settlements, and foraging in surrounding fields. Sometimes extremely pale-coloured individuals crop up among the normally plumaged birds.

Rooks forage throughout the farmlands at all times of the year, but appear in great winter concentrations, often in association with jackdaws. Their pre-roost winter flocking around stubble fields is often a source of great interest to road users as highly vocal gatherings blacken both sky and ground at their favourite meeting places. It is such apparently sociable meetings that have resulted in countryside notions of crows' 'weddings' and the like.

Starlings do farmers a service in ridding grassland fields of leatherjackets, the damaging underground larvae of 'daddy longlegs'. Winter sees large groups of starlings ranging over the Black Isle countryside. These are probably immigrants, and no doubt include some of the birds which crowd the ledges of buildings on winter nights in the centre of Inverness, creating

The scent of meadowsweet fills the summer air along overgrown farmland ditches.

something of a hazard for pedestrians passing below!

Wild geese also descend in winter flocks on to the farmlands surrounding the firths. For the most part these gatherings consist of greylags, feeding by day on grain stubbles and grass fields, then flying off to roost on the upper firths by night. Pinkfooted geese are less commonly seen on the farmlands, although huge flocks may be seen, and bean geese put in an infrequent winter appearance.

Though the visits of wintering goose flocks may be viewed with mixed feelings by farmers, they are an expression of the way in which, through time, wildlife has increasingly been forced to come to terms with a largely man-managed Black Isle countryside.

CHAPTER 6
Cairn and Castle

A glance at the Ordnance Survey maps which cover the Black Isle will quickly reveal that the peninsula is rich in historical remains. Indeed, the whole area is a good illustration of the geographer's idea of the landscape being like a palimpsest, an old piece of parchment used many times over, where fragments of previous correspondence still show through. So it is with the Black Isle countryside, where reminders of human activity in the past endure in the landscape of the present.

But a more detailed look at the map will reveal that there is some pattern in the apparent random scatter of remains. If the survivals from the most ancient human past are plotted against the pattern of the relief, a distinct concentration is apparent on the higher Mulbuie and on some of the smaller areas of high ground. Why should this be?

The answer may have less to do with the pattern of today's countryside than with the one which existed in the past. It should be remembered that the productive farmlands of today were won by immense human effort from badly drained and frequently wooded low ground. In ancient times, then, to folk unable to rise to the challenge of drainage and woodland removal, the central ridge with its great expanse of heather moorland offered more potential than the lower ground. The pattern of today's human landscape may, to a large extent, be the reverse of how things were long ago. In terms of present day farming, the central core is seen as highly marginal, and, as a result, much of it has been planted in forest.

So who were those shadowy folk of the past who raised up the great stone cairns which survive today? Sadly, their life and times are a bit of a closed book. Only the scantiest evidence remains to help piece together any kind of picture of their way of life. Doubtless they were hunters, for arrowheads have been found, and doubtless they kept livestock, too, on the open expanses of moorland ground.

Faced with what seems, to the layman, like a mixed bag of cairns and tombs, archaeologists have classified them into

The Grey Cairn is an ancient reminder of the prehistoric folk who once wrested a living from the higher areas.

distinct groups. The Black Isle appears to be something of a transition zone between the two main types of tomb. To the Orkney-Cromarty group, typical of the area to the north, belongs Carn Glas near Mains of Kilcoy farm in Killearnan parish. Its twin apartment chamber and passage have been excavated and some leaf-shaped arrowheads found.

To the Clava type, characteristic of the area to the south, belongs nearby Cairn Irenan, a passage-grave. The name Clava is derived from an area with a distinctive grouping of cairns just to the south of Inverness and close to the Great Glen. There is little doubt that this major natural routeway was once an important means of communication from the west coast to the eastern Highlands. Largest of all Black Isle cairns is the Grey Cairn behind the farm of Glenurquhart on the main road to Cromarty, but little has been learned of its history or of the ancient folk who once felt moved to create it.

A number of cist burials laid bare by plough or spade at various times give the Black Isle a link with the whole of the eastern seaboard of the north. Cists consist of flat slabs of stone forming a rude coffin, in which a skeleton is generally found reposing on its side in a crouched position. Alongside is a beaker, a fairly large pottery container in which food was placed, perhaps for the journey to the after life. There have been two particularly good early Bronze Age beaker finds, one recovered from a cist in the garden of Rosemarkie Manse in 1904, well decorated with whipcord impressions, and another uncovered in a mound in 1941 during wartime operations at Blackstand. These have been dated to the period between 1800 and 1400 B.C.

In common with other areas, some of the most enduring landscape relics are of a defensive nature. The need for protection was clearly an important fact in early people's lives, and a good illustration of this is the Iron Age hill fort on top of the forested Ord Hill of Kessock. This contains evidence of vitrification where interlaced timbers must once have burned so fiercely that the stones have formed a fused mass. By contrast, duns were smaller scale defence works represented by a number of examples. One dun site is near Culbokie, another lies on the side of Drumderfit Hill above Munlochy Bay, and a third is not far away, overlooking Loch Lundie.

Although in popular terms, earliest human history tends somehow to be equated with cave-dwelling, the fact is that caves as a form of residence were in fairly short supply. In this respect, however, the Black Isle was quite well endowed, and there has been a long tradition of cave inhabitation. In contradiction of the popular idea, however, excavation of the cave that lies beyond Rosemarkie revealed no evidence of earliest man in the area. Instead, the shell midden which stands at the cave entrance yielded up some worked pieces of bone and antler, along with a ball and pin of post-Roman age. The exact date is uncertain, but is thought to be somewhere in the period 200 to 800 A.D. In fact, cave occupation persisted into recent times, though residence was usually of a fairly temporary nature by what would today be called travelling folk.

From our perspective in time, there are great gaps in the early historical record. But life went on, and we must assume that succeeding generations lived out their lives in an uncomplicated relationship with the land, dwelling in homes that were an extension of their surrounding environment, for they were fashioned from materials which the land provided. A few examples of hut circles exist here and there, for example beside the dun on Drumderfit Hill, but these are only vague ground markings of what would once have been family homes.

Sometimes the evidence of the past may be much more intriguing. At some stage before construction of the present parish kirk of Rosemarkie, a superb sculpted block of sandstone was recovered from the foundations of the previous building. For years, this has been a source of fascination and pride to local folk. But the Rosemarkie Stone, as it came to be called, was more than just a tribute to the skills of some long departed masons. In time, it furnished valuable evidence of Rosemarkie's participation in the Pictish past.

Several other fragments of stonework have been recovered from the same area. They include one found in the kirkyard with a representation of a beast attacking a man. One suggestion is that it might be a representation of Daniel in the Lions' Den. Another shows the lower part of two men wearing long tunics with decorated hems and carrying spears. It seems likely that the complete figures would have resembled the trio of tall, kingly figures featured on the Pictish symbol stone from the Brough of Birsay in Orkney. Other fragments have recently been transferred from Rosemarkie Church, where they lay unremarked upon, to the museum at Groam House on Rosemarkie High Street.

Fascinating though these Pictish stone fragments are, none can match the appeal and attraction of the Rosemarkie stone itself. On its face there is a wealth of intricate carving. It is described as a Class II Pictish cross-slab with zoomorphic decoration. Put more simply, it depicts various strange beasts, as well as the characteristic double disc, crescent, Z and V rod symbols, and of course the inscribed cross. No opportunity should be missed to see this classic stone and the explanatory material which accompanies it within the museum. With the aid of spot lighting, all the intricate details of its complex design may be clearly traced. There can be little doubt that the presence of this, and all the other relics of the enigmatic people who bequeathed us the symbol stones, places Rosemarkie firmly on the map of Pictish Scotland.

In due time came the building of the castles and keeps whose well fortified walls ensured their survival into today's landscape. One of the most significant of these remains is the imposing, sixteenth century Craig Castle which sits on a rock outcrop on the shores of the Cromarty Firth, below

C

Cullicudden and not far from the bridge. Even as a ruin it is an impressive remain, looking out across the tidal firth to the distant hills of Ross and Sutherland.

Built in the late sixteenth or early seventeenth century, this fortified tower belonged to the Urquharts of Cromarty, though it was afterwards occupied by the Bishops of Ross. In later times, it found a use which might well have raised a clerical eyebrow. The place became a well known centre for illicit whisky distilling at a time when this was a widespread Black Isle pastime. Not very far away are the traces of Kinbeachie Castle, another tower house associated with the Urquhart family.

Of the castle at Cromarty nothing now remains, though there are some old drawings to give a good idea of how it looked. It was demolished in 1772 when the present Cromarty House was built in its place. It also had been erected by the Urquharts, and is believed to have dated back to the thirteenth century. The name of Castle Street in Fortrose similarly recalls a fortification that is no more, though Fortrose Castle is believed to have been built as a towerhouse at the beginning of the sixteenth century.

Ormond Castle, on a firthside hill beside Avoch, is a more identifiable remain, though little now remains of this once important fortification with a history that spans the twelfth to the sixteenth centuries. It was a stronghold of the powerful De Moravia family in the thirteenth and fourteenth centuries. In 1297 it was held by Sir Andrew de Moravia, and formed a rallying point for patriots. Sir Andrew was killed at the battle of Stirling Bridge. His son, Andrew Moray, was regent during the reign of David II. He died at Avoch, as recorded in the old stanza:

> 'Oure the Mounth than passit he
> Till Avawch in his awyne cuntre,
> And thare then endyt he his dayis
> As before the Cronkyll sayis.'

Later, Ormond Castle was held by the Douglas family, Earls of Ormond. Local tradition has it that the stones were removed to be employed in the construction of Cromwell's fort in Inverness.

Craig Castle looks across the Cromarty Firth to the hills of Easter Ross. Once an imposing fortress, the castle is now a crumbling ruin.

On the shores of the Beauly Firth, in one of the most attractive corners of the Black Isle, stands the gaunt ruin of Redcastle. These are the crumbling remains of a grand mansion house built by the laird last century, but the historical significance of the place lies much further back. Tradition has it that this is the site of the Castle of Eddyrdour, built by William the Lion in the twelfth century. There is some earlier history attached to the present nineteenth century extravaganza, however, for it incorporates part of a sixteenth century fortified tower house.

The Black Isle countryside sports two inhabited castles. Kilcoy Castle in Killearnan parish is a four-storeyed tower house of Z plan. Originally constructed early in the seventeenth century, Kilcoy has been extensively renovated in recent times.

Kinkell Castle, in a commanding position overlooking the head of the Cromarty Firth just outside Conon Bridge, was erected in the late sixteenth century for John Rory Mackenzie, a chieftain of the Clan Mackenzie. Time and neglect later reduced the once fine building to a state of decay. During the eighteenth century it was converted to a country house, and by the beginning of the present century had the status only of a farmhouse. Kinkell was rescued from a state of severe neglect in 1968 by its present owners who have extensively renovated the building.

By the time of the First and Second World Wars, castles had long since lost their role in the defence of the realm, but in unsettled times the need for fortified defences still remained. At the entrance to the Cromarty Firth may still be seen the concrete pill boxes from which heavy guns could be trained on the water below in case of enemy attack. Though many would question their historical value when set aside the ancient castles of the Black Isle, they are surely as much a part of the history of the peninsula as those more ancient survivals. As such, they have their own place in the Black Isle palimpsest with all its varied reminders of the past.

CHAPTER 7
Kirk and Kirkyard

Kirks, and the kirkyards which surround them, invariably have an interesting tale to tell. No journey around the Black Isle would be complete without a look at some of them at least, for within and without their old walls you may frequently discover much about the people's past.

It would be easy enough to spend a whole day on a Black Isle 'kirk trail'. For those who might choose to do so, this chapter is presented in an order which will, hopefully, serve as useful background to a round trip of the ecclesiastical riches of the peninsula.

Taking the main road from Inverness and turning down towards Munlochy, the first obvious church is the one which stands on the left, beside the tree nursery at Bogallan. This pleasant sandstone building with its little neat tower is Knockbain Free Church, built just over a century ago. After the Disruption of 1843, when many ministers left the established church to form the Free Church of Scotland, several fine sandstone places of worship were erected throughout Easter Ross and the Black Isle. They were often located some distance away from the nearest settlement and parish kirk, for they could only be built where land was made available, and the lairds generally supported the established kirk.

From here the view is to distant Ben Wyvis and across the fertile farmlands around Allangrange House. A short detour from Munlochy will allow a glimpse of a church ruin of a very different type and age. Allangrange Chapel is dedicated to St John and distinguished by a triple lancet window of thirteenth century date.

A few more miles along the main road, the spire of the parish kirk of Avoch rises from the trees on the wooded brae above the fishing village and the firth. The present building, in nineteenth century Gothic revival style, replaced one constructed around 1670, itself the successor of a medieval foundation.

One feature of the building is of particular historical significance. Set into the vestry wall is a sacrament house or decorative aumbry, thought to date back to the beginning of the sixteenth century. Nothing is recorded of its origin, nor indeed of the church in Avoch in those early days, though it is known that in medieval times the parish kirk had been appropriated by the powerful Cistercian Abbey across the Moray Firth at Kinloss. The sacrament house is a rare survival, for, apart from one at Contin in Ross-shire and another at Kirkwall in Orkney, there are no more examples north of the Moray Firth.

High in the bell tower is another survival from the past. The old bell carries on its side the appealing inscription 'Mine name is Anna'. In the kirkyard below, the gravestones bear the names of generations of fisher folk. Amongst the most poignant memorials are those to the women of the village who perished in a terrible accident just offshore. Though it happened in the summer of 1871, the tragic impact of 'The Drooning' was to cast a shadow over the lives of many Avoch families right into the present century.

The tragedy occurred when some women were being ferried out to the boat which was to take them to Inverness to sell their fish to the town housewives. A sudden swell caused the small boat in which they were being rowed to toss about. Panic set in. Fearing for their safety, the women rushed to one side, causing the boat to overturn and pitch them into the sea. The accident took a terrible toll. No fewer than fourteen women perished, some leaving young families behind. The gravestones in the peaceful burial ground outside the kirk tell their own sad tale of this devastating event.

Though the fisher folk of Avoch existed with the constant threat that the sea could take away as well as give, for the most part they lived their lives within the predictable rhythms of a small fishing community. The same could hardly be said of Avoch's most famous resident who lies buried in a plot alongside the kirkyard wall. Sir Alexander Mackenzie settled at Avoch House in 1812, after his epic journeyings through the unexplored wastes of Northern Canada. His name is commemorated in the mighty Mackenzie River which flows northwards into the Arctic Ocean. In recent years, some

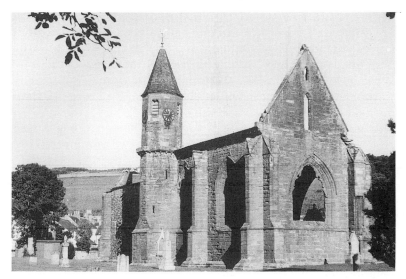

The cathedral kirk of Fortrose, the ancient Chanonry of Ross. This fine red sandstone building is only a portion of the original structure.

Canadian wellwishers, anxious to keep alive the memory of his achievement, provided some funds for the upkeep of his grave.

For centuries the cathedral kirk of Fortrose must have been a great focus of worship. Time has not dealt kindly with the once great building, but its remaining red sandstone magnificence still has the power to draw the visitor to wonder at the skills of the masons who shaped it out of raw rock hewn from Black Isle quarries.

The oldest remaining part is the detached two-storeyed range. It dates from the thirteenth century and has had a varied history of use down through the ages. Originally the ground floor was the meeting place and sacristy of the cathedral chapter. The treasury was upstairs. After the Reformation, an outside stair was added. The ground floor became a prison, while the upper floor served as burgh court room and town council chamber.

Sadly, the complete cathedral does not survive. The remaining part is merely the handsome aisle said to have been added at the behest of Euphemia, Countess of Ross, in the later fourteenth century. She was the victim of an unfortunate marriage with the notorious Wolf of Badenoch.

The ground pattern of the original cathedral is now marked out in stone chippings. Only by tracing the outline of this area does one begin to grasp the true scale of the original building. What is left today, then, and what many visitors mistakenly consider to be the cathedral itself, is a mere portion of what must once have been an impressive structure.

A walk around the outside walls of this remaining South Aisle will give some idea of the enormous labour involved in the cathedral's construction. Perhaps it is the evening light which shows it to best advantage, when the slanting rays of the setting sun catch the red blocks and impart a warm, mellow glow.

Close study of the stonework will reveal the patterns of ancient river flow mentioned in the first chapter, and visitors should look also for the mitred heads of bishops carved on the exterior, though many are now badly weathered. But it was not only the masons who left their marks on the outside stonework. Grafitti are not confined to the present age. Various initials have been incised into the stonework of the cathedral in the past, in differing styles of script, and on one block there is a small inscribed caberfeidh, the stag's head symbol of the Mackenzies.

Such scant respect for the fabric of the old building clearly extended also to the bell tower, for among the weathered pock-marking on the stone may also be seen the rounded impressions left by the impact of musket balls. The old bell which hangs inside the tower continues to ring out the nightly curfew as it has done for generations.

Those who came on horseback had some assistance provided for mounting and dismounting their steeds. The 'loupin-on stane' of grey gneiss can still be seen today in the midst of the old gravestones outside the cathedral walls.

Unfortunately, the beautiful sandstone wall of the south side has been spoiled by the insensitive placing of a modern polished granite slab. The interior of the south aisle has suffered the same fate over the years. The flat sandstone slabs on the west floor are spared the ravages of outdoor weathering, but now suffer the constant wear and tear from visitors' feet. Although imported white marble could hardly be

The old kirkyard of Kirkmichael beside Udale Bay. The ancient gravestones bear the names of families who continue to live and work the surrounding land today.

said to blend easily with the native red sandstone, the marble memorial tablets which line the interior walls do reflect some of the social history of this part of the world, and its associations with the once great Seaforth family is well emphasised.

The walls carry the marble memorials to the Seaforth Mackenzies. The extraordinary tablet on the west wall is that of Sir Kenneth Mackenzie, supposedly showing himself in death overlooking Redcastle, his seat on the shores of the Beauly Firth. Other features of the interior are the impressive workmanship of the vaulted roof and tombs of early bishops topped by carved stone effigies. Doubtless it was the vaulted nature of the roof of the Chapter House and South Aisle that saved both from ruin.

When workmen broke into one of these tombs in the late eighteenth century, they discovered a wooden bishop's crozier. Believed to have been the symbolic staff of Bishop Cairncross, one of the sixteenth century bishops of the cathedral, the relic is now in the National Museum in Edinburgh.

The exact circumstances of the ruin of the cathedral are

uncertain. Tradition lays the blame on the shoulders of Oliver Cromwell's troops, on the lookout for convenient supplies of prepared building stone for their fortification in Inverness. The true picture, however, is probably one of gradual dilapidation.

After the Reformation, little interest would have been taken in the maintenance of the old building. Indeed, the process must have been considerably speeded up by removal of the roof. In 1572 it is recorded that Lord Ruthven was granted 'the hail leid quharwith the cathedral kirk of Ross is thickit'. When Cromwell's men did remove the sandstone blocks, it was probably from what was already a ruinous building. A well known engraving of the Chanonry of Ross three hundred years ago shows the place to have been in the same state as it is today.

A short walk from the cathedral is the pale sandstone building of St Andrew's Scottish Episcopal Church. After Presbyterianism became established in Scotland, Episcopalians became hard pressed. Lady Louise Turner, in her little history of the church in Fortrose writes of the Episcopalians being 'plunged into a constant struggle to maintain their ways. Undignified squabbles between clergymen were not uncommon: fisticuffs, sticks and stones from congregations unwilling to have a Presbyterian, or as it might be, an Episcopalian 'intruder', were the order of the day.' Things really had come to a pretty pass when, in 1707, the Presbyterian minister at Rosemarkie took away the keys of the church, forcing the Episcopalians to make shift and worship where they could.

In 1790, a feu was granted for the present building which stands on the braehead overlooking the firth. When opened in 1827, the church had services in both Gaelic and English to suit the needs of the congregation of the time. Though Gaelic preaching has long disappeared, the congregation continues to flourish, and present day visitors to Fortrose will enjoy spending a few restful minutes within the beautiful interior of St Andrews Church.

Although uncertainty surrounds the location of early ecclesiastical foundations at nearby Rosemarkie, there is no doubt about the age of the present building. While Fortrose may have overtaken Rosemarkie in importance a long time ago,

The preaching burn at Ferintosh. Here, some of the finest churchmen in the north once preached to crowds assembled in this natural amphitheatre.

the building at Rosemarkie remains the parish kirk.

It first opened its doors for worship in 1821. The parish minister of the time, the Reverend Alexander Wood, had succeeded his father and died after a ministry spanning sixty-five years. Both his father and grandfather also had long parish ministries at Rosemarkie, as the observant eye will note outside in the kirkyard.

The exterior has recently been extensively renovated. Visitors to the church will find an attractive, traditional country parish kirk interior. However, the front vestibule may well be of greater interest for the collection of church bygones which it houses. These include an early pewter cup and bread patten for use in communion services. The well-used lead communion tokens are dated 1786 and bear the parish name 'Rosemarky'. They are typical of the tokens once carried by communicants to permit them to participate in the sacrament.

In an age when the preaching of the Word was invariably a lengthy business, the large hour glass was an indication to the minister (and doubtless also to well-positioned members of the congregation) of how time was passing during the preaching of the sermon. And when the sands of time had finally run out for any of his parishioners, the mort bell was solemnly rung by the grave-digger on the last earthly journey from house to grave.

Much too valuable to be kept in the church is a beautiful old Scottish silver communion cup. It was gifted to the church by the Countess Isabella of Seaforth in 1686, and despite its great age is still in occasional use. The vessel is engraved in Latin on one side with the donor's name. On the other appears the text from First Corinthians, Chapter eleven: 'Let a man examine himself, and so let him drink of this cup'. A set of photographs of this interesting link with the parish past is available for view in the church vestibule.

Apart from the roll of names of those who left the parish to fight in the First World War and never returned, there is another reminder of war in a distant land. The plain and worn soldier's testament which now reposes in the peacefulness of the church was carried throughout the campaigns in which he fought by General Sir Richard O'Connor, a former member of the kirk session at Rosemarkie. During the Second World War, General O'Connor served as a commander under Montgomery who said of him: 'I have a great and real affection for Dick; to me he is the salt of the earth and one of the elect'. Now, far removed in time and place from the chaos and carnage of two world wars, the soldier's testament has been given a final home in this quiet corner of the Black Isle.

Echoes of strife in a far off place are also in the kirkyard. Perhaps the most interesting of these is the memorial to Dr Brydon, C.B., sole survivor of the bloody British retreat from Kabul in January 1842, during an earlier Afghan conflict.

Elsewhere stand the old sandstone memorials to the folk who formed the fabric of parish life in days gone by. Farmers, fishers, shoemakers, bakers, lighthouse men and their families all lie side by side. They were the folk who served one another in times when parish life was self-contained and interdependent in a way that it is not now. A summer evening stroll among the old stones is a way of meeting with the changing parish past, set against the background of the timeless surge of the sea on the shore down below.

In the East Kirk of Cromarty, the Black Isle and the north have an outstanding example of an early reformed church. In 1582, the first presbyterian minister was ordained, shortly after the building's construction. It has therefore had a remarkable four centuries of Christian witness.

From the road, it is an unpretentious, two-storeyed T-shaped building. The Rev. Robert Galloway has written: 'Because this church does not architecturally force itself on the landscape but lies behind the long white wall in Church Street many visitors, particularly motorists, may pass what is perhaps, one of the architectural gems of the 16th to 17th century in this town. The history and tranquillity which one encounters . . . carries the soul into another realm and another age'.

A strong feature of the old kirk is the survival of the three lofts. Facing the pulpit is the Poor Loft where the poor folk of the parish sat. The Laird's Loft housed the family and servants of the laird of Cromarty, while the Scholars' Loft was occupied by the village dominie and his charges.

Other features of interest are the arms of the Ross family who were lairds of the Cromarty estate, and a lozenge-shaped funeral hatchment of the type once displayed at the burial of a person of status, covered with heraldic devices. In more recent times, a memorial was erected inside the church by the Saltire Society to Sir Thomas Urquhart of Cromarty who won international fame as translator of Rabelais, and is popularly said to have died of a fit of laughter on hearing of the Restoration of the Monarchy.

At one time, the parish of Cromarty had chapels or churches, dedicated to St Duthuc, St Bennet and St Regulus. At nearby Navity Moor it was widely believed that Judgement Day would take place. In fact, so strong was this belief that a local man in dispute with another requested that he be buried outside the kirkyard of St Regulus so that he might be first to meet his Maker. This unusually positioned grave can still be seen outside the fence. Also in St Regulus kirkyard is the underground burial vault of the Ross family, and the simple little headstone carved by Hugh Miller to mark the grave of his infant daughter.

The Gaelic Chapel, immediately obvious to the visitor entering Cromarty from the east side, was built at the end of the eighteenth century to serve the spiritual needs of Gaelic speaking workers brought in to Cromarty in the eighteenth century by the laird to work in his various manufacturing enterprises. Last used as a place of worship by Polish soldiers during the Second World War, the building is now roofless.

A little further to the west, the parish of Resolis may seem a quiet enough place these days, but there was a time when dramatic ongoings there brought the place to the notice of the outside world. It happened in the wake of the 1843 Disruption mentioned earlier. The Rev. Donald Sage, minister of Resolis, now a minister of the Free Kirk, was left without a building in which to preach – a not uncommon situation throughout the north at that time. Services were held beside the firth in an old rent barn which had once stored the meal and grain collected by the laird in the days when rents were paid in kind.

When the new clergyman (who was the choice of the local heritors) was about to be introduced to his parishioners, a crowd gathered at the kirk door determined to prevent all access. The authorities, however, had somehow got wind of the planned disturbance, and a detachment of redcoats was marched over from Fort George.

Despite the presence of the military, the local folk jeered and booed the lairds and their new man. Then, when things really began to heat up and stones started to fly, the order was given to fire (with blank cartridges). This act served only to incense the rioters further. The soldiers then determined to make an example of one of the agitators by seizing a woman from the crowd, bundling her into a gig and heading for Cromarty jail.

There she was duly incarcerated, but rescue was soon at hand. In the evening, a crowd of Resolis men arrived in Cromarty determined to bail out their unfortunate kinswoman. When bail was refused, tempers flared once more and with a rush at the door, the jail was broken into and the prisoner released. Such were the on-goings which shattered the peace of the Highlands in those controversial times.

In the aftermath of the Disruption, preaching in unconventional places was not uncommon. Worshippers in the rat-infested barn on the firthside at Resolis at least had the advantage of a roof covering over their heads. Those who gathered in the valley of the burn at Ferintosh had to take the

Among the unconventional preaching places in the aftermath of the Disruption of 1843 was a rent barn on the shore of the Cromarty Firth near Cullicudden.

elements as they came. There, beside the old oak trees of Drummondreach with their carpets of woodland flowers, the people gathered in a natural grassy amphitheatre carved by the rushing burn. In this unconventional setting the finest church men in the north once preached to immense crowds of open air worshippers.

Amongst the best known was Dr Macdonald, 'Apostle of the North,' most popular of all Gaelic preachers of his time. Shortly after his arrival as minister of Urquhart, Macdonald's wife died. Refusing to have the impending communion service postponed, the minister went out and preached to an extraordinary gathering on the communion Sunday. It was an age when worshippers would travel many miles to attend such a service, and on this occasion the congregation was said to number thousands. Of the atmosphere that attended such gatherings, the Rev. Thomas Brown, chronicler of the 1843

Disruption wrote: 'When the vast audience were seen hanging on the lips of the greatest preacher in the north, and fairly moved by his stirring appeals, the whole scene was such as no one who witnessed it was ever likely to forget'.

A little further along the firth, close to the muddy bay of Udale, lies the ancient parish kirk of Kirkmichael. Only a ruin now remains, but the kirkyard contains the graves of many of the families of the district. Centuries removed in time from the ancestors whose names are inscribed on the mossy sandstone slabs at Kirkmichael, some of the old Black Isle families, like the Holms of Ferryton, continue to live and farm in the area today.

Their link with the past is part of recorded history. The lives of countless past Black Isle generations have been slowly forgotten with the passage of time. Such was the case at Newhall Point, where a shoulder of land juts out into the firth. Apart from the name Chapelton applied to a nearby site, there was nothing to suggest that anything remained from the place's distant church connection. Nothing, that is, until 1985 when a digger excavating a new house site at the Point disturbed some human bones. All further work was immediately stopped until a rescue 'dig' could be carried out by archaeologists.

As the digger's trowels began to scrape away at the almost pure sand below the top layer of soil, a whole group of well-preserved human skeletons was carefully laid bare. Local interest in the find was intense, but one particular interest in the corpses seems to have been especially so, for in the dead of night two of the best preserved skeletons were mysteriously spirited away never to return.

After laboratory tests in Edinburgh which concluded that the bodies were part of a Christian burial ground dating back to the eleventh century, presumably at the site of the lost chapel, the parcel of bones was duly returned to the place from which they had come. In a simple ceremony, the parish minister of Resolis and Urquhart committed the remains back to the Black Isle soil in which they had quietly reposed for centuries till they were rudely disturbed.

A tour of Black Isle kirks and kirkyards might be brought to a pleasant end by a visit to the ruined parish kirk of Urquhart which stands right on the Cromarty Firth shore. With the background sounds of the birds on the mudflats below, this is a pleasant place to stop for a while beside the ivy-covered walls. Here repose the earthly remains of Dr Macdonald whose preaching once fired the north. It has been claimed that this peaceful spot is the site of the martyrdom of St Maelrubha. But whatever its history, like so many other places, Urquhart Old Kirk and its encircling kirkyard are a tangible and fascinating link with the Black Isle's human past.

CHAPTER 8
Forming the Farmscape

The Black Isle countryside as we see it today is largely the product of farming change. To understand the extent of that change, it is necessary to go back from today's farmscape to yesterday's countryside. As elsewhere in Scotland, the run-rig system had dominated the rural scene for centuries. Small fermtouns, consisting of a huddle of houses and steadings, were surrounded by improved land which lay in scattered patches among tracts of unreclaimed ground. Crops were grown in long strips or rigs, and, in the absence of fences, livestock were herded to prevent them straying on to the cultivated areas.

For the most part, crops were grown as part of a subsistence way of life in which the people largely lived off what they grew and reared. The more productive areas were able to furnish a surplus which found a ready outlet through the port of Cromarty. In addition, there was one part of the Black Isle where the product of local farming could be consumed on a large scale. Using locally grown barley for malt, the name of

The Young family harvesting at Ness Farm just after the Second World War. The era of the Clydesdale horse was soon to give way completely to that of the combine harvester. (Photograph courtesy of Miss H. Young, Ness Farm).

the district of Ferintosh became synonymous with whisky production generally. Indeed, as output increased, so the population of the area rose as people moved in to engage in the thriving distilling trade. Thanks to an apparently insatiable demand for the product of a multitude of stills, the folk of Ferintosh had never had it so good.

It had come about in this way. As compensation from the Government for losses sustained as a consequence of his loyalty during the Jacobite unrest, Forbes of Culloden, who owned the Barony of Ferintosh, was in 1689 granted the privilege of whisky distilling without Government excise duty. The implications of this were enormous. Distilling brought boom times to Ferintosh, since the product could undercut anything being produced anywhere else. A hitherto obscure Black Isle district name became a household word throughout the country. Local barley growers found a market on their doorstep, and a distillery was built to supplement the output of the abundant small stills in what was one of the best known Highland cottage industries ever.

But all good things must come to an end, and in 1786 the Government was moved to revoke the Ferintosh Privilege as it was known. Such was the impact of the news of this decision that Robert Burns refers to it in a poem penned almost immediately afterwards. In 'Scotch Drink', he writes:

> *'Thee, Ferintosh! O sadly lost!*
> *Scotland, lament frae coast to coast!*
> *Now colic grips, an' barkin' hoast*
> *   May kill us a';*
> *For loyal Forbes's chartered boast*
> *   Is ta'en awa'!'*

In fact, low prices were probably already causing problems for the distillers, and in any case it was perhaps just as well for the Black Isle countryside that the whole thing was doomed to disappear. The demands being made on available fuel to fire the stills was resulting in widespread removal of trees and even threatening the farmlands, as surface turf was ripped off in a desperate attempt to keep the still fires burning.

It has often been assumed that the lairds alone, with their

available capital and awareness of progress in other places, were to be the real force for change in a long-established agricultural system which might feed the folk in most years but could produce little by way of surplus for sale. Yet, a good example of improvement wrought by a Black Isle tenant has recently been brought to notice. In the Proceedings of the Society of Antiquaries of Scotland, H. Gordon Slade has noted how the 1746 plan of a survey of the farmlands of Mickle Pharnes at the Cromarty end of the Black Isle shows only the cluster of buildings that was the fermtoun.

A new survey in 1764, however, shows not only the unplanned huddle of buildings of the Meikle Farnes fermtoun (note how easily place-names can change), but a well-organized group of farm buildings at a site called Allartoun, closer to the Cromarty Firth. This was a well-planned farm complex resembling the improved style of larger farms of the time. But what makes it more interesting is that it was the creation of one Kenneth MacCulloch, a tenant on Mickle Farnes. Unfortunately, this progressive tenant was not fated to enjoy the fruits of his labours, for, at a time when rents were largely paid in kind, a series of bad harvests together with a high outlay on the improved buildings pushed MacCulloch deeply into debt and cost him his farm tenancy.

Elsewhere in the Black Isle, the hand of the landowners in shaping the face of the countryside is still widely seen. Elaborate steadings, such as those at Raddery, Tarradale and Newhall distinguish the home farms of the lairds. The gentlemen farmers who conceived their grand designs dominated the lives of the country folk who worked the land around them, and who brought their payments in kind to the lairds' rent barns which were built along the Cromarty Firth. Payment was usually in grain, but live hens invariably featured also, till the change to money rents last century.

In the pattern of farming improvement, certain landowners came to dominate the Black Isle scene. After extensive land acquisition, Fletcher of Rosehaugh owned no less than ten thousand acres, expending great effort in drainage, fencing and general land reclamation. High class pedigree shorthorn and Aberdeen Angus cattle grazed the Rosehaugh farmlands, and it was clearly in the interest of the laird to see that their

Today's farmland patchwork is the legacy of yesterday's farming improvers who laid out the pattern of the fields.

good qualities were transmitted to the tenants' stock as well. At the far end of the peninsula, Ross of Cromarty similarly dominated the farming scene. The services of high quality stock bulls were available at a set fee, and at the same time impressive Clydesdale stallions were travelled from district to district to raise the quality of working horses on the farms.

On the larger estates, new farm buildings were being widely constructed in the second half of the nineteenth century. The sandstone-built houses of the Rosehaugh estate are a particularly striking tribute to this phase of the Black Isle's rural history. The Rosehaugh laird also responded to a need for educational provision in the landward area by building the school and schoolmaster's house at Killen which match closely the style of the improved buildings of the farmlands round about it.

The patriarchal, and often patronising, interest which the big landowners took in the folk who worked their lands is seen in surviving accounts of harvest-home celebrations and the like. For example, the local newspaper reported that in October, 1880, the tenants and servants of the Cromarty estate were entertained by the laird in the large granary above the Cromarty House stables. 'The place was very tastefully decorated with evergreens, flags, etc. In the centre overhead was an emblem of 'Harvest Home' – oats and barley in the form of a square and compass. In the adjoining end, tables were set and loaded with good things for the supper. Dancing was commenced at nine o'clock, to the lively strains of bagpipes, on arrival of a distinguished party from Cromarty House.'

It was an age when every Black Isle laird seemed to have an insatiable thirst for land reclamation. Eyes were inevitably turned on the Mulbuie Common, the long, dark elevated spine of moorland which had for so long dominated the face of the land. By Scots law, the Mulbuie was held to be in common to the estates, however, and not to the ordinary folk. By an earlier Act of Parliament, the legislation for commonty division already existed. Now this vast expanse was allotted to the adjoining proprietors. The Royal Burgh of Fortrose also claimed a portion, and was duly rewarded with its own tract. Naturally, the largest landowners stood to gain most from this share-out, but there was a host of much lesser claimants, too, including ministers of the kirk, by virtue of their holding of the glebe lands which provided much of their living.

All in all, about forty different land owners of widely varying importance were involved. In fact, commonty division was a real blow to the ordinary country and burgh folk who looked to its bleak acres to supply them with fuel for their fires, thatch for their roofs and grazing for their livestock. In addition, turf was pared from the moor and burned to ash as a form of fertiliser for the fields. Stones were gathered and quarried for building purposes, and clay was brought home for cottage walls and floors. In short, the Mulbuie Common provided people all over the Black Isle with many of the essential needs of the time.

It was the practice of some estates to move crofters gradually upwards as they improved the lower lands. In this way, some of them had come to settle on the bleakest ground at the very top of the Mulbuie, thinking that on such common land they would not be subject to any landowner. But this did not prove to be the case, and when the commonty was divided up in 1828, the settlers on the Ferintosh portion of the Mulbuie were immediately subject to an initial nominal payment of one hen. The ill feelings caused by increases in rentals on the land of Forbes of Culloden were brought to light in evidence given to the Crofters' Commission of Enquiry held in Dingwall in 1883.

Clearly, this rough grazing land of the old common had potential for better farming use, but that potential could only be realised with a massive input of human labour. As it happened, a source of labour could be obtained without too much effort. The clearances which were making way for sheep in the inland straths were being achieved at the expense of the folk who lived there. Large numbers of evicted crofters from Strathconon in particular were settled on Black Isle land which was in need of reclamation, establishing a pattern of smallholdings which can easily be traced at the present day.

As the Mulbuie Common slowly yielded to the plough, the encircling skirt of green advanced slowly inland and upwards. Perhaps the transformation was best summed up by James Macdonald, writing of the farming in Ross and Cromarty in 1877 in the Transactions of the Highland and Agricultural Society of Scotland. 'The improvement these reclamations and plantations have effected on the scenery of the Black Isle is very marked', he noted. 'Before the division a dark dreary shade was cast over the whole peninsula by the bleak heathy moor, which then ran along the ridge; now the many green fields and thriving plantations that occupy the greater part of the old Mulbuie, lend a pleasant, smiling aspect to the whole district.'

There was also some potential for reclamation at the heads of the firths. The extent of firthland reclamation may be seen in the pattern of embankments and flat fields at the head of the Beauly Firth near Tarradale, and at Munlochy Bay. But while envious eyes were long cast across the saltmarshes and mudflats, most of these areas were to remain untamed.

During the second half of last century, farming progress was widespread throughout the peninsula. New crops and supporting fertilisers were raising the productivity of the farmlands. Newspaper advertisements of the time list an impressive variety of clovers and improved cereals and roots on offer. Some were to be a success, others to fail. Time-consuming visits to the seaside to cart unpredictable supplies of seaware up on to the fields could be dispensed with as suppliers of bone meal, South American guano and other manures began to promote their products.

But it was not all complete innovation. There was scope for improvement using more traditional sources. In the 1870s, for example, Mr George Middleton, a member of a most progressive farming family originating in Yorkshire, was carefully managing the use of natural, organic fertiliser on his farm of Davidston near Cromarty. His system was to feed large numbers of cattle indoors in summer on cut grass and cattle cake so that the dung could be made available for use on the fields where and when required. It seems that the modern concept of zero-grazing may not be so modern after all!

At the same time, Mr James Gordon was sowing large amounts of whins on his farm of Udale. Present day Black Isle farmers, so intent now on ridding their lands of whin, may raise their eyebrows at the very suggestion. Yet, one of the Udale fields involved no less than twenty-two acres of whin sowing. The softer, fresh shoots were cut by mower, then crushed in an Irish whin mill made before feeding to cattle, horses and sheep. It was reckoned that the production of this crop on such a scale allowed a larger number of livestock to be kept. Furthermore, the whins actually improved the land by breaking up the hard pan in the soil.

Elsewhere, an onslaught was taking place on the whins and broom which grew in profusion on the unimproved land. In the 1870s, the Rosehaugh estate was advertising for a force of human grubbers to tackle the work. The same advertisement also sought contractors to lay out new roads and to drain large tracts of standing water and bog land. Yet, despite the change and progress going on, the old ways persisted with the new for a long time to come. While improved cereal varieties began to dominate the arable lands, rye continued to be grown as a material for thatching houses and outhouses.

Inevitably, a degree of competition existed among the bigger farms. This found some practical outlet in the ploughing matches which drew enormous crowds in the slack winter months. Fortunately, these were always well reported upon in the local newspapers, so that we may form a good idea of what things were like at these popular events.

Greenside Farm. The fine sandstone and slate buildings erected late last century are often of little relevance to today's needs. The outside stair leads to the granary, once a characteristic feature of Black Isle farms.

In March, 1884, for example, the Cromarty District Ploughing Match took place on the farm of Navity belonging to the Cromarty estate. On this occasion, the estate itself could muster no fewer than fifteen pairs of working horses for the event. There were prizes for grooming and harness, as well as ploughing. Special prizes were awarded to the youngest ploughman, the tallest ploughman, and the ploughman blessed with the greatest number of daughters.

The laird dispensed hospitality in the form of unspecified refreshments for the ploughmen on what was a cold and raw winter's day, but it is clear from previous match reports that drinking and ensuing rowdyism could be a problem at these events. No doubt it was in response to this that the Blue Ribbon Army had set up its tent in the Navity field, providing a more temperate beverage (coffee) to supply warmth to the inner man without firing his more arguesome spirits.

The great wealth of Fletcher of Rosehaugh also allowed him to indulge in a livestock enterprise that was outwith the mainstream of horse breeding. Starting with two black mares brought over from the island of Rhum, Fletcher proceeded to build up a stud of Highland ponies which was to become renowned throughout the country. The best known pony ever to be foaled at Rosehaugh was Jock, an animal destined to receive worldwide attention as much loved mount of King George V. At Sandringham and Balmoral, Jock was the King's favourite pony, and, at the end, was to lend a poignancy to the royal funeral procession which was long remembered. As the gun carriage with its flag-draped coffin passed the silent crowds, the grey Black Isle pony, with empty saddle, walked quietly behind.

The ploughing matches with their big displays of working horses provided an opportunity to demonstrate the latest in improved ploughs and the wonders of steam ploughing. But it was not just among the bigger farms that improved tillage was being demonstrated. By 1890, Mr MacLennan of Rootfield, well known for his progressive approach, had not only introduced the reaper and steam mill into his district, but had instituted the Land League ploughing match and was doing much to improve the standards of ploughing on the nearby crofts.

By the end of the century, the lines of the Black Isle farmscape as we know them today had largely been drawn. Stone dykes and wire fences marked off field boundaries which have persisted to the present day. Only here and there, are vague remnants of the old feal or turf dykes to be seen. Fortrose golf course is a good place to look for them, especially when the evening sun throws into relief the subtle patterns of a past farming landscape.

In fact, echoes of the past were to persist on Chanonry Ness right up to the present time. Partly as a result of the existence of ancient mortifications and endowments for the upkeep of the burgh poor, the old rigs of the poor's lands continued to exist when the farming lands round about were totally reorganised. The Seaforth rigs, for example, were established for the upkeep of the needy poor by a mortification of the Countess Euphemia of Seaforth in 1680, and only recently have they been swallowed up into the present pattern of land ownership.

Old names like Rye Bank and Thorny Cleatie survive on Chanonry Ness as reminders of an extraordinarily late example of land fragmentation that recalls the farming countryside as it would once have been. Although amalgamation has now removed the old pattern, in certain conditions from the Hill of Fortrose the marks of old rig boundaries may be picked out on newly ploughed land.

Apart from this odd surviving relic, the twentieth century farming landscape of the Black Isle came to reflect the mixed nature of its farming economy. The ubiquitous farm steading, with outside steps leading to an upper granary, recall days when oats were the essential fuel of the farm workforce, providing fodder for horse and feeding for horseman.

Inevitably, the changing trends in agriculture of more recent times have imposed their own demands on the face of the countryside. Drainage and reclamation have continued on a reduced, but significant, scale, to the detriment of surviving remnants of natural habitat. Fortunately, nothing came of an ambitious scheme proposed in the 1970s to create vast areas of polder farming land in place of the present expanses of Beauly Firth mudflats. Field size has increased in many places, allowing use of the largest implements and machinery. Fences have totally disappeared around some fields, as a complete emphasis on arable farming has dispensed with the need for stock fencing.

Unfortunately, with the disappearance of the livestock has gone the important input of organic fertiliser which had always helped maintain soil structure. Not surprisingly, on a number of large sloping fields, soil erosion has appeared as a new and disturbing phenomenon. In recent years, heavy rain has promoted a downward flow of valuable topsoil and nutrients, resulting in a network of rills and small gulleys on a scale never seen in the farmlands of old. Roadside ditches have become infilled, and road surfaces covered, as a result of an environmental problem which has emerged throughout the intensive arable lands of North-east Scotland.

Lack of livestock on farms has also resulted in reduced demand for straw as bedding. The result has been the all too familiar straw burning of autumn which pollutes the atmosphere with its pall of acrid smoke.

Dairy farming has always played a subsidiary role to beef cattle production in the Black Isle. Nevertheless, dairying continues on a limited scale. Black and white Friesians and Holsteins now take the place of the native brown and white Ayrshires in a style of farming that reflects advances in automation and the application of science to livestock husbandry.

Elsewhere, pure-bred cattle are rarely seen. The stamp of the Continental beef breeds is evident everywhere. Black Isle farmers of the old generation have witnessed a dramatic swing away from the use of native shorthorn, Aberdeen Angus and Hereford bulls towards those of the imported Charolais, Simmental and Limousin breeds. Here and there, small numbers of the old native Highland cattle are occasionally maintained, a source of great attraction to passing summer visitors.

To provide winter livestock feed, grass cutting for silage has become dominant, though hay making continues as a widespread summer activity. Gone are the days of laborious forking and turning, however, and even the small square bales of not so long ago have yielded to the mammoth round creations of today's automated countryside.

The manual art of turnip hoeing is seldom now required as precision sowing has taken over. But turnips still play an important role in feeding those sheep which are brought into the Black Isle in the autumn from hill lands to the west where winter feed is scarce. It is a practice which has been engaged in by generations of Black Isle farmers and crofters, and its continuation is a reminder of the seasonal movements of livestock once widespread in upland parts of the country. In the past, the sheep flocks were walked across or brought in by rail. Now cattle floats decant their baaing contents into fields whose fences must be well maintained to enclose animals which have spent the summer roaming free among the hills.

Although it is to be assumed that whisky distilling is a lost Black Isle art, it is to the distilleries of the North-east that Black Isle farmers have looked in recent times for a market for their malting barley. The result has been a great emphasis on barley

Symbol of the decline in rural self-sufficiency, the meal mill at Munlochy now stands empty, its water wheel slowly crumbling.

production to the complete exclusion on many farms of oats, the old time staple cereal crop. Wheat continues to be grown on the bigger farms, and oil seed rape really made its presence known on a large scale in the 1980s, with vast expanses of vivid spring yellow punctuating the green of the farmlands.

To a large extent, the attractive countryside of the Black Isle today is the outcome of how landowners and tenants of the past formed the farmscape and used those areas which defied farming use. The urge to press every possible piece of ground into agricultural productivity has resulted in an almost total loss of the once widespread wetland and moorland areas. Perhaps there may be some hope for increased diversity in tomorrow's countryside in a recent suggestion that agricultural support may not be given if it is at the expense of the rural environment. But old ideas die hard, and an old Black Isle farmer on hearing this suggestion, asserted 'They'll be asking us to leave a band of weeds round every field next!'

CHAPTER 9
The Black Isle Show

For thousands of visitors each year, the Black Isle has come to mean only one thing – the annual summer show. Held on the first Thursday of August, the Black Isle Show is the premier one-day agricultural event in Scotland. Surrounded by the display of high technology machinery and all the other attractions, visitors might be forgiven for assuming that this highly popular occasion is a product of the modern age.

In fact, nothing could be further from the truth, for the show (strictly the Black Isle Farmers' Show) has had a long and illustrious history, making an important contribution to land and life in the Black Isle since its early inception.

To understand the origin of the show, it is necessary to appreciate the need for agricultural improvement which existed at the beginning of last century. Much has been written in recent times on the exact nature of Scottish farming improvement, but whatever the overall Scottish picture, at a local level the role of the small farming improvement societies as a force for change has not always been given its fair due.

The importance of the Black Isle Farmers' Society in hastening farming progress in its own area is clearly revealed in the pages of the Society's minute books. As was the pattern of things elsewhere, the impetus to form such a farming society came from the local landowners, though they had in mind the spread of ideas of improvement throughout the whole Black Isle farming community.

Some uncertainty surrounds the exact date of origin of the society, but at a gathering of the leading local landowners in Fortrose, in March 1836, it was resolved to institute two annual meetings in the Black Isle burgh. The latter of the two, to be held on a Thursday in October, was to be the forerunner of the present Black Isle Show. Since the Society was formed to become involved in the 'promotion and interests of agriculture', those earliest shows were to become both a mirror of the best in local farming, and a reflection of improvements taking place more generally throughout the northern farming districts.

All ready for the show ring. The class for dressed Clydesdales has always been a popular attraction at the Black Isle Show.

No doubt there would have been great excitement in the normally quiet Black Isle burgh that October day when the best of the farm animals of the time were walked in from the surrounding countryside and stanced on the Cathedral green of Fortrose. There was no shortage of interest for this inaugural event, for the secretary noted that 'the show of horses, black cattle, sheep and pigs was larger than can have been expected in consequence of the backwardness of the harvest'.

The following spring saw the introduction of an annual competition for seed and root crops, again establishing a tradition that has continued to the present day. The earliest seed and root classes present an interesting picture of varieties of crops being grown at the time, with prizes on offer for Hopeton, Angus and potato oats, barley, beans and peas. From the very beginning there was an air of progressiveness about the Society, and one can easily imagine the enthusiasm among the gentlemen members as they met at a local hotel to dine after each show, no doubt keenly anticipating the next.

No sooner were these earliest shows past than decisions were being made on classes for more crop varieties and livestock breeds for future events. New classes were established for white wheat and shorthorned cattle. Members resolved to form themselves into 'parochial committees to act in their respective parishes and to use every means for promoting the success of the object, and to request the cooperation of their clergymen and elders'. With the combined power of landowner, minister and kirk working to promote the improving ideas throughout the peninsula, the Society was clearly set to be a force for change both in agricultural output and in the whole farming landscape.

Early discussions centred on matters of land improvement, especially drainage. At one Society meeting in the 1840s, Captain Sutherland of Udale was able to offer advice to his fellow members on the value of forming large field drains using small stones gathered off the land. As a result, 'the meeting were almost all of opinion that small stone drains in the district would be found most economical and advantageous'. At the same gathering, members resolved that a ploughing match should take place the following spring.

The perennial question of how to tackle the crows and rooks which foraged over the farmlands was answered by the decision to raise a levy among the members of half a crown for every plough, the purpose being to create a fund from which bounties might be paid for every bird destroyed in the rookeries during the breeding months.

By the fifth spring seed and root show, 'it was apparent to what perfection agriculture has been brought in the Black Isle. Indeed it would be difficult to find finer samples of seed grain than exhibited on the Cathedral green of Fortrose.' A satisfying confirmation of the value of these shows came at the 1843 spring meeting. Mr Middleton of Davidston, one of the most progressive farmers of the area, was able to tell his fellow members that he had 'that day purchased no less than 120 quarters of seed grain from the samples shown at the competition'.

As the spirit of farming improvement became more widespread during the 1840s, members aired a wide variety of topics. Discussions ranged over matters such as the most effective way of using guano (imported South American seabird droppings) and the best kind of oats from the different soils of the Black Isle. The spring shows introduced new premiums for the best potato varieties currently being grown, for sandy oats and rye grass, and, significantly, at the summer show some of the premiums awarded earlier for Highland cattle were withdrawn in favour of others for 'first crosses from the Shorthorned bull' and for animals of the 'Aberdeen polled breed'.

Members were not slow to address social questions when appropriate. Almost at the society's beginning, they had considered the destitution that prevailed over on the West Coast, and resolved to form a committee 'for the purpose of providing assistance for their unfortunate countrymen in money, grain, meal and potatoes'. More than anything else, perhaps, this gives some indication of the advances being made in Black Isle farming, throwing into even sharper focus the tremendous contrasts between east and west in terms of agricultural productivity.

The Black Isle Farmers were not the sole organised force for farming change in the area. Across the Cromarty Firth, the East Ross Farmers' Society mooted the idea of a combined cattle show at Invergordon, but the Black Isle Farmers rejected the suggestion, citing the impractibility of shipping cattle across the Cromarty Firth with its unpredictable tides and water conditions. On a wider canvas, however, livestock transport by sea was an important matter for northern producers, and in 1849 members heard at first hand from a representative of the North of Scotland Steam Packet Company about proposed new services that would help put the north in better touch with southern markets.

By the 1860s, the show pens reflected the mark being made by the Black Isle in improved livestock breeding. Shorthorn cattle began to dominate the cattle scene, and several local breeders possessed fine stock obtained directly from Sittyton in Aberdeenshire, where Amos Cruickshank had brought the Scottish shorthorn to a level of development undreamed of only a few decades before. Fletcher of Rosehaugh and Cameron of Balnakyle were both taking along to Fortrose some purebred shorthorns of first class quality, the latter gentleman on one occasion 'carrying off the chief honours with an animal of gigantic proportions'.

With new varieties of potatoes and other root crops constantly being introduced, classes at the spring show had frequently to be modified. Small-scale poultry keeping was always a feature of the farming countryside, and this rather neglected sector was not being overlooked when the larger livestock were assembled for show. Here was an opportunity for those not into the big league of larger livestock breeding to gain a coveted prize ticket. Poultry classes encouraged the showing of 'turkeys, geese and ducks, Dorkings, Spotted Hamburghs, Black Spanish and Brahmapootras'.

In 1881 the livestock show was changed from an October date to one in August, a time which suited the farmers better because it came before the busy harvest period. By now, the summer show was attracting so much interest that the secretary was instructed to 'correspond with the Chief Constable and ask him to provide a sufficient force of men for the occasion'. Soon, entertainment for the crowds was also being provided by pipers engaged to play throughout the day, and the colourful attraction of a pipe band continues to be a popular feature of shows to this day.

By the 1890s, the summer show had significantly grown. Its increasing reputation as a window on Black Isle farming was now drawing farmers and crofters from miles around. The large attendance of wives and families, and the increasing numbers of non-farming folk from the local community was creating a demand for some alternative entertainment on the big day. To some extent this need was met when the summer shows were moved to the Rosehaugh House policies outside Avoch, for the general public were allowed the rare opportunity of gazing (no doubt in awe and wonder) at the exotic vegetation in the magnificent Victorian palm houses and conservatories.

This was now an era when the showing of Clydesdale mares was in the ascendancy, a reflection of the advanced state of horse breeding within the Black Isle at the time. But if the cattle classes had been dominated by the superior pedigreed livestock of the more affluent proprietors, the Society minutes record with interest that Mr Colin Munro of Tullich, something of a pioneer of improved horse breeding in the

Dressed for the hills. The parade of garrons in working gear is a great draw for visitors to the show.

Black Isle, was a comparatively small tenant farmer who 'time after time gave farmers of the north the benefit of his stud on very reasonable terms'. His Clydesdales were said to be 'of rare breeding and quality'.

Of course, the larger proprietors maintained fine studs also, and one of the benefits of Society membership as far as the smaller tenants were concerned was that Mr Fletcher was willing to provide the services of a quality Rosehaugh Clydesdale stallion free of charge to fellow members. Not surprisingly, in this period of great interest in showing work horses, a competition for shoeing was instituted, adding the strong smell of singeing horse hooves to the atmosphere of the summer show.

By the ending of the century, the reputation of the Black Isle Show had certainly been established. By 1894, the *North Star* newspaper could record in its columns that the summer show was 'far and away the best ever held by the Society. We go

further and state that no other district in Scotland of the same
area could produce so many animals of such undoubted merit
as were here exhibited. The district is fortunate in the
possession of a number of tenant farmers who are second to
none in professional 'go' in any agricultural district in Great
Britain.'

The same columns reported in 1896 that on show day 'the
trains were crowded with visitors, while the tidy little screw
steamer *Rosehaugh* carried its fair quota'. The show had gone
from strength to strength at Rosehaugh, but in 1899 it was
back in Fortrose, at the request of the Town Council. The
Black Isle Show was now enjoying a reputation as a display of
some of the best shorthorns and polled cattle anywhere in the
country. At the same time, the non-farming aspect was being
strengthened, the band of the 3rd Batallion the Seaforth
Highlanders crossing over from Fort George to entertain the
crowds.

Donkey races were a novel feature of the 1906 show, and
there was an unusual opportunity to extend the competitive
spirit of the sporting events. For sailors from the many
warships gathered in the Cromarty Firth the Black Isle Show
was able to provide some welcome shore diversion.

The *Inverness Courier* reported that the 1908 show held in the
recreation park in Fortrose was notable for a 'display given by
the tars and marines from HMS *Ringdove*'. A large crowd
journeyed to Fortrose by train on that occasion also, and the ss
Nellie had to make a special trip to cope with the extra traffic
generated. The minute books make little comment on the
weather enjoyed on show days, but the *Northern Chronicle* for
1910 noted that 'The annual stock show at Fortrose was held
under very depressing circumstances, for the rain never
stopped, making everything look bad and feel worse'.

Perhaps it was somehow prophetic of the mood of times to
come. Certainly the presence of the large numbers of sailors
from the Cromarty Firth at previous shows had been a bad
omen, for the 1914 minutes poignantly record that Sir John
Fowler, Captain and Adjutant of the 4th Seaforth Highlanders
had brought to the members' notice the case of Alick Jack,
Littleburn, asking the Society 'to see to the securing of his
harvest and attention to his stock during the time he is serving

his King and Country'. In 1915 members resolved that there should be no summer show, and this was to be the pattern for three more years while so many Black Isle men were away on active service.

If the spring seed and root shows had tended over the years to be eclipsed by the reporting of the summer event, it was not for lack of interest or quality. In the early years of the century the gardeners at Rosehaugh were able to stage an impressive display of no fewer than twenty-five different potato varieties. Nor were the smaller livestock sections short of supporters at the big show, either. By the 1920s there were classes for Rhode Island Reds and Wyandottes in the poultry section, a reflection of the greater interest being placed on improved egg production from these American imports.

Proceedings at the 1928 show were enlivened by a competition for the 'best dressed motor car'– a prognostication of things to come, since the idea was clearly suggested by the long-established decorated horse class. There was also a lively competition for catching the greasy pig, for some reason restricted to ladies only. But things were far from lively in the farming scene at the time, and members were evidently feeling the pinch, complaining of high charges by blacksmiths and mill owners at a time of falling farm prices. In 1934, crisis point seems to have been reached, and a general meeting was held to discuss whether a show should be held at all, and in the event of it being decided not to hold one, to discuss the advisability of winding up the Society.

It would have been a great pity if such an illustrious institution had been allowed simply to fade away at this point in time, after its great contribution to the Black Isle's farming development. Fortunately, there were enough members who cared about the Society's continuing future to ensure that the unthinkable never happened. For a while the show returned to its Rosehaugh House venue, and in 1936 a class was added for dairy cows, reflecting the improvements being made in that sector of the local livestock industry. The following years saw greatly reduced numbers in the shorthorn and Aberdeen-Angus classes, however. Yet the minutes observe that work horses were still strongly represented, 'proving that they are not all being ousted by mechanisation in the Black Isle'. As war clouds gathered in 1939, the summer show was improved by the use of a public address system, but though the seed and root shows continued, the summer show was temporarily suspended till more settled times might come again.

Those days were eventually to return, but it was to be a full ten years before the summer show could be revived. In a happy post-war atmosphere, a day of perfect weather drew a record show crowd to Munlochy Mains farm. After all the uncertainties of the past, it was a great day out. On a field overlooking the nearby bay and the sparkling waters of the firth beyond, an astonishing five thousand people walked among the lines of livestock pens and trade stands.

There were some problems to overcome, however, due to post-war shortages. Wood was scarce, but 'the organisers overcame the difficulties of obtaining timber permits for erecting pens and enclosures by improvising in such a skilful way, that although the work involved was increased tenfold, the ultimate layout showed no sign of having been faced with the agony of restrictions'.

In the cattle classes the native Scottish breeds reigned supreme. The Ayrshire section was strong, as was that of the Aberdeen-Angus, and the supreme trophy for most outstanding exhibit in the cattle section went to a fine shorthorn bull, Bapton Upright, belonging to Captain James Cameron of Balnakyle. In 1953, however, the Society minutes mourn the death of Captain Cameron, one of the great links with the heady days of the past when Black Isle shorthorns reigned supreme. Captain Cameron had brought credit to the Society abroad when he was accorded the rare honour of being invited to judge shorthorns in Argentina.

Attendance records continued to be broken as the show moved on circuit around several Black Isle farms, but the last 'show on the road' came in 1955 when six thousand people converged on Tore Mains farm. All subsequent shows have been held on the permanent site at Mannsfield, Muir of Ord, near the place where the drovers of old had stanced their hardy Highland cattle in times past. Over the years, the decision to locate on a permanent showground was vindicated time and again as crowd numbers grew.

But if the outward face of the Black Isle Show had changed,

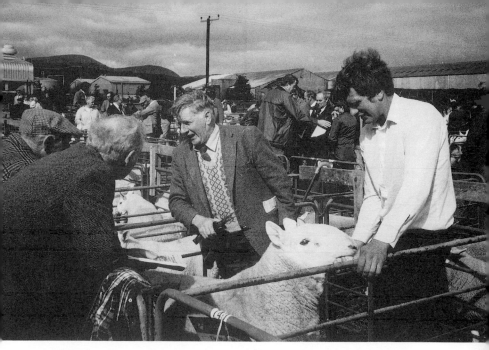

Just time for a quick blether as the Cheviot tup is prepared for the show ring. Cheviots from as far away as Caithness compete for the honours in the sheep classes.

the essential character of a compact, one-day event remained, and has continued to this day. As the expanding array of trade stands came to reflect the changing trends in farm mechanisation, the numbers of work horses gradually dwindled away, though the day of the show Clydesdale has come again, with increasing entries in the heavy horse classes during the 1980s.

In 1986, the Black Isle Show celebrated in style its 150th anniversary year. Appropriately, the guest of honour on that occasion was Her Majesty Queen Elizabeth the Queen Mother, whose North Country Cheviots from her Castle of Mey estate in Caithness have frequently featured in the sheep pens.

Though the Continental cattle breeds, particularly the Charolais, Simmental and Limousin, have ousted the once dominant native beef shorthorn, 'the blacks' can still muster a show, and Highland cattle never really faded out of the picture at all, despite several gloomy predictions. In the dairy cattle section, however, the native brown and white Ayrshires have given place to the higher-yielding Friesians and Holsteins,

Continental breeds now dominate the show pens, but a few native Highland cattle still make an appearance.

which, in turn, are now simply classed together as black and white dairy cattle.

The revolution in livestock breeding has embraced the sheep classes also, with the introduced Texel, Vendeen and Bleu de Main breeds making a show, and the spotted Jacob sheep becoming a firm favourite with non-farming visitors. Goat numbers have greatly increased, a reflection both of an expansion of hobby farming and the general trend towards small-scale rural self-sufficiency. The rare breeds, too, have put in an appearance, with striking long-horned cattle, diminutive black Dexter cattle, and four-horned black Hebridean sheep all providing a reminder that the old time breeds, though low in numbers, are not lacking in their own supporters.

With the need for diversification in agriculture becoming ever more apparent, red deer have recently been exhibited in a well-fenced enclosure by one of the deer farms which now exist throughout the north.

Things have come a long way since those first Black Isle Farmers gathered together on the Cathedral green of Fortrose to show off the best of their stock on that October day in 1836. Black Isle Show day has become something of a local holiday, with many businesses shutting down so that their staff can attend.

On a well-drained natural site overlooked by croft-studded hills and distant mountains, crowds from miles around converge each August to enjoy a fine day out in a pleasant setting. Attendance figures have soared to a staggering twenty-seven thousand. A vast array of entertainments now accompany the traditional heart of the show – the livestock pens and associated agricultural trade stands. There, animated groups of farmers take delight in arguing the finer points of a Holstein heifer or a Texel tup, carrying their good-natured discussion over to the well-patronised refreshment tent where the drams flow as freely as any Black Isle burn.

Yet, despite all the change and innovation over the years, the essential spirit of the Society lives on, and the much-loved Black Isle Show goes from strength to strength, a credit to its organisers, and a continuing tribute to the vision and drive of those early Black Isle Farmers.

CHAPTER 10

Patterns of Travel

Until the bridging of the Cromarty and Inverness Firths, the Black Isle enjoyed, or suffered from, depending on different viewpoints, a high degree of insularity.

Yet, in an age of poorly developed road communications, the waters of the surrounding waters used to link up firth-side communities in a way that they do not do now. There was a time last century when it was possible for Black Isle travellers to be picked up by one of the coastal steamers which plied the east coast route, linking northern ports with Leith in the south. At the same period, travellers from Fortrose and Avoch could avoid the time-consuming road journey to Inverness by embarking on one of the little firth steamers such as the *Speedwell*, the *Nellie*, the *Rosehaugh* and the *Eilean Dubh*.

The volume of shipping in the firths early last century was justification for the building of two lighthouses, one at Cromarty and the other at Chanonry Point. The work of constructing these similar lights fell to the famous Stevenson lighthouse building family. In interior design they were a wonderful tribute to their builders, fitted out with shining brass and adorned with the head of Alexander the Great, builder of the first great lighthouse, the Pharos at Alexandria. These two fine Black Isle buildings are no longer open to the public.

Although by mid-century it had two lighthouses to guide shipping in the firths, the Black Isle was not particularly well blessed with harbours. Those at Fortrose, Cromarty and Avoch are small and suffer the problem of siltation. At one time, Fortrose harbour did have a long extension jetty, but this has long gone. The main use of the harbour today is for recreation, with a large number of sailing dinghies moored offshore in the summer months.

The local sailing club has its base at Fortrose harbour, beside the old quayside store which used to house cargoes brought in from small trading ships entering the harbour. Apart from that, there is only one other relic of the days of flourishing coastal trade. An ancient crane, once used for lifting bulky

The Kessock ferry, 1978. Though replaced by the Rosehaugh as the main boat, the Eilean Dubh continued to operate as relief vessel right to the end of the ferry service in 1982. The ferry operated between the pier at South Kessock, Inverness, and that at North Kessock on the Black Isle (seen here in the background).

cargoes, now finds a modern use for hoisting dinghies out of the water at the end of the sailing season.

Cromarty harbour sees little shipping activity these days, apart from some recreation and small boat fishing. Up until 1968, however, it was the R.N.L.I. lifeboat station. From the establishment of the station in 1911, with a boat called *The Brothers*, Cromarty men rendered illustrious rescue service, a fact commemorated inside the East Kirk. Now the lifeboat which serves this part of the coastline is stationed across the water at Invergordon.

Avoch's harbour continues as home base for the local fishing boats which can enter only at high tide. In fact, they are seldom at home, the crews usually travelling by minibus to fishing ports on the west coast. In the late 1970s, there was some revival of interest in coastal trading at Avoch, when a Black Isle coal merchant received supplies directly from collieries in the north of England by way of a small coaster, and in 1980, bales of straw were dispatched northwards by coaster to Orkney stock farmers hard-pressed after a disastrous summer.

Around the coast lie a number of disused jetties once important in exporting building materials from the peninsula's sandstone quarries. On the Beauly Firth there is a small pier below Tarradale House from which sandstone was shipped out

99

of the adjacent Tarradale quarry. Further downstream is the long protruding jetty at Redcastle, from which blocks were removed to form the walls of Telford's Caledonian Canal. On the north side of Munlochy Bay lies the quarry where shallow-draughted ships called to load stone for the building of Fort George in the middle of the eighteenth century, an operation which must have greatly boosted the volume of shipping in the firth.

One of the most important of these sandstone loading jetties was at Findon, near the place where traffic using the Cromarty Firth bridge now leaves the Black Isle. By good fortune, a mid-eighteenth century account survives of the shipping activities centred on Findon quarry and pier. It describes a hive of activity, with as many as six large ships loading stone. To service the needs of this flourishing trade, no fewer than twenty-two quarriers, seventeen masons, thirty-nine labourers and a smith were in employment at the quarry at the time.

Today, not a single sandstone working quarry remains in the Black Isle. The once bustling piers lie disused and dilapidated, crumbling contributions to the industrial archaeology of a place now more widely known for the reputation of its farming than of its fine building stone.

Road transport was rather ill-developed until comparatively recent times. When the Black Isle branch railway line from Muir of Ord to Fortrose was opened in 1894, it provided a much improved means of handling the Black Isle's outgoing produce. The primary products of the land were transported for shipment to southern markets. Such was the volume of the Black Isle's cattle trade, for example, that the railway terminus at Fortrose had a separate siding where cattle were loaded into special livestock trucks.

The Black Isle's other branch line was begun in the early part of this century but never completed. Planned to run from Dingwall via a crossing of the firth narrows at Alcaig ferry to a terminus in Cromarty, construction of the track was commenced from the Cromarty end. A locomotive to assist in track laying was laboriously hauled across country using a traction engine, so at least it can be claimed that a train actually ran on the line, but all the effort was to be in vain. The country was thrown into war, and all work stopped. Although the track of this abandoned branch line and some bridge work can be traced between Cromarty and Jemimaville, detail of this incomplete chapter in the communications history of the Black Isle has largely faded from local memory.

By contrast, the Muir of Ord to Fortrose branch line railway did create significant local employment, in operating the trains and stations and in track maintenance. The little row of railway workers' cottages at Fortrose still survives in the middle of a modern housing area, the station area having been cleared and redeveloped.

The railway also carried passenger traffic. But in the post-war era the writing was on the wall for the network of branch lines like the Black Isle railway which had been constructed in the age of railway mania. Competition from road transport finally killed off the Black Isle railway, the last passenger train running along the line in 1951, followed by the lifting of the track in the early 1960s.

Little now survives as a reminder of this closed chapter in the history of Black Isle communications. A few buildings, such as the station master's house, some bridges and disjointed sections of embankment are all that remain of the Black Isle branch railway.

The physical geography of this part of the Eastern Highlands imposed real disadvantages for the communications network. The mainstream of north-south communication along the east coast was badly disjointed by the Black Isle's surrounding firths, so that travellers were dependent on a once substantial number of connecting ferries.

Even today, some of the names on the map of the Black Isle commemorate the well-established presence of these ferries long after their demise. On the north side, where crossings of the Cromarty Firth were comparatively short, ferry links existed at Alcaig, at Alnessferry in Resolis and a short distance away at Inverbreakieferry at Balblair.

Unfortunately, little detail of the day-to-day running of these ferry services survives from the past. Only the untoward or bizarre was considered worth recording. For example, readers of the *Ross-shire Journal* shared in the astonishment of the onlookers at the Invergordon ferry pier over on the other side on an October day in 1877. They had watched, helpless, as a horse, yoked to a cart, decided for reasons best known to itself to go for a swim out into the firth, cart and all. Unfortunately, the unusual exertion proved too much, and the poor beast expired before it could be persuaded to return from its adventure.

More conventional movement of livestock across the intervening waters could also create problems. Enormous spirited Clydesdale stallions, for example, on their travels around the countryside last century, had to be coaxed and cajoled into boat crossings. And there was always the question of cost. In 1887, Black Isle farmers were pressing to have tariffs on the Kessock Ferry reduced from their existing level of 'ox, cow or heifer 6d; sheep, lamb or goat 1d; small pigs in bags 2d'.

In the heyday of industrialisation along the northern side of the Cromarty Firth in the late 1970s, the ferry crossing to Invergordon continued to be operated by a passenger launch from the pier at Balblair, but without heavy subsidy such services are hardly viable in this age of speedy road communication, and this old-established crossing is now no longer used on a regular basis.

Travellers along the old east coast route were traditionally dependent on two ferry crossings. On the Inner Firth, a regular service between Fort George and Chanonry Point was maintained until 1932 when the last regular ferryman died. Passengers unlucky enough to be caught in the maelstrom of tides and currents which churn the waters between those narrows must often have had a long and harrowing passage. Small wonder, then, that an inn was conveniently placed at the very end of Chanonry Ness to which storm-tossed travellers might retire with all haste as the boat decanted them on to the slipway.

The old ferry inn which once dispensed drams to drenched and travel-weary travellers survives, though now converted to a private house. Set into its seaward gable is an intriguing little round window which gave a good view of the outer firth and any travellers caught up in its tide-rip. When horses used to be stabled at the inn, care had to be taken that they were not frightened into panic by the sudden flash of the adjacent lighthouse beam.

Generations of travellers, from the most humble to the mightiest in the land once made this important crossing of the firth. It has been termed the 'Royal Route' because James IV was one of a steady stream of pilgrims northwards to the shrine of St Duthac at Tain. But the Chanonry crossing was a great leveller, and king and commoner alike had to commit their lives at this point to the skills of the boatmen who maintained the ferry crossing and knew the ways of those troubled waters.

After a comparatively short land journey across the eastern end of the peninsula, travellers bound for northern destinations were subjected to the further rigours of the Cromarty to Nigg crossing. Interestingly, this is the only one of the old Black Isle ferry links to have survived. When the oil platform construction yard became established at Nigg in the 1970s, the Black Isle men employed at the base were transported across the narrows by a small passenger vessel.

With the fluctuating fortunes of the yard, and periodic declines in its labour force, maintaining a regular crossing created some problems. In an attempt to maintain a direct ferry link with the northern side of the Cromarty Firth, a new, purpose-built boat, the *Cromarty Rose,* was introduced on to the crossing, capable of accommodating two cars as well as passengers. In addition to maintaining a direct connection with the developments across the firth, it was felt that a ferry might also help tourism in the area, allowing a round trip from Inverness through the Black Isle to Cromarty, then back along the Easter Ross coast road.

The main ferry link in recent times was the one across the Kessock narrows, linking the Black Isle with Inverness. Corresponding piers were constructed at South and North Kessock, and a succession of varied craft shuttled across the entrance to the Beauly Firth. In more recent times, however, purpose-built vehicle ferries maintained the vital connection.

Post-war years saw the arrival of the sturdy *Eilean Dubh,* carrying the name of a previous firth steamer. By dint of much manoeuvering (a traumatic experience for many an unwary visitor), up to eight cars could be accommodated. The increasing number of foot passengers from Kessock, many of whom were Black Isle commuters leaving their cars in the ferry car park, sought refuge from the soaking salt spray in a small inside cabin. In time, the *Eilean Dubh* had a companion on the crossing. The *Inbher Nis,* named after the Highland capital, had a turntable deck and accommodated four cars, but could offer little in the way of passenger comfort.

In 1967, a buzz of excitement spread through the Black Isle. A brand new and much bigger boat had been delivered from the Fairmile yard at Berwick-upon-Tweed. By comparison with her trusty old predecessor, the *Rosehaugh* seemed positively sumptuous. Travellers quickly got used to the new vessel with her straight-through car deck, allowing vehicles of all sizes to drive on at one end and off at the other. During early morning and late afternoon runs, the *Rosehaugh* also carried a fair complement of bicycles belonging to those who risked the journey on two wheels into work in the centre of Inverness.

The 'new boat' (for as such she was known long after her delivery) gave good service during her days shuttling back and fore across the Kessock narrows, before heading up river to her night-time berth. The *Eilean Dubh* was retained as a relief vessel, but in latter years her reappearance when the *Rosehaugh* went out of service for her annual refit was greeted with widespread horror. To arrive at the ferry pier and discover that the *Eilean Dubh* was back on duty, and to see the lengthy queue, was frequently to turn and make an immediate start on the long detour round the Beauly Firth, a major headache when in a hurry to catch shops or offices in Inverness before they closed.

The tourist season was a time of particular trauma as one sat in the ferry queue trying to judge if the car and caravan in front would take up all of the remaining space, or whether there might be just enough room for one more car, thus saving a half hour wait till the boat made her next crossing. Invariably, the ferry men did their best, however, and if there was any hope of squeezing one more on board they would edge everyone else up a few centimetres more until the car was safely in position and the ramp just managed to shut.

In the last few years of the ferry service, major frustrations began to build up among regular users. The poor old *Eilean Dubh* was really feeling her age, and finding it difficult to cope when required to stand in for her successor. In the end, after a series of malfunctions and break-downs, she was uncharitably

Sole survivor of the many Black Isle ferries, the Cromarty-Nigg passage is served by the Cromarty Rose (left). This crossing survives largely because of the presence of oil-related industry in the Cromarty Firth.

nicknamed the 'Ailing Doo', which, as any good Scot will know, has nothing to do with Gaelic, but is a description of a sickly pigeon.

The idea of bridging the two firths had been conceived in an atmosphere of optimism regarding development of the Eastern Highlands. While a low span design was satisfactory for the Cromarty Firth crossing, a high-level suspension design was required for the Kessock Bridge to allow the passage of ships to the harbour at Inverness. Now, with the bridging of the Dornoch Firth further to the north, the pattern will be complete, and the saving in time on journeys from Caithness and Sutherland to the Highland capital considerable. An obvious consequence of the bridging of the firths was the construction of a new section for the A9, the main road route to the north. This now gives travellers a brief introduction to the Black Isle as they cross the peninsula between the Kessock and Cromarty Firth bridges, but does have the disadvantage of bisecting the peninsula.

The Cromarty Firth Bridge was first to be completed. When it was opened, a large volume of traffic to and from the north began to cut across the Black Isle rather than use the long detour route around the head of the Beauly Firth. At critical times, ferry queues became frustratingly long, and many people who would otherwise have regretted the passing of the ferry service looked ever more anxiously for the closing of that final section on the growing Kessock Bridge.

The new structure was modelled on a bridge spanning the River Rhine near Dusseldorf. When, in 1983, the final gap was at last spanned and traffic began to flow, many Black Isle travellers breathed a deep sigh of relief. On being stood down from service, the *Eilean Dubh* travelled over to the Cromarty Firth to act as a tender for the oil rigs moored there for service and repair. For a brief moment, at the very end of her career, she found the fame which had been denied her in a lifetime of humble shuttling back and forth across the firth. When a well-preserved wartime Wellington bomber was raised from the murky depths of Loch Ness, the *Eilean Dubh* appeared on national television as the diving support ship of the much-publicised recovery project.

The *Rosehaugh,* with more years of service left in her, also travelled down through the Caledonian Canal, as replacement boat for the Corran Ferry. Householders along the main road at North Kessock, used to the frantic, last-minute dashes for the departing boat, could now enjoy more peaceful days as the once busy ferry crossing point readjusted itself to a new role as quiet residential village.

Though few would deny the advantages of greater accessibility to services which the passing of the Kessock Ferry has brought, there were bound to be some regrets when the *Rosehaugh* finally severed her connection with the Black Isle. After a journey away from home, there was always a certain satisfaction on the return crossing as the ramp went up and the bustling world of the Highland capital was exchanged for the quieter charms of the Black Isle.

Gone are the pleasant mill-pond winter crossings with their close-up views of goosander and guillemot breaking the mirrored winter reflection of snow-covered hills. Gone, too, are the grandstand views from the top deck of the *Rosehaugh* of dolphin couples leaping from the water in amorous unison.

With the passing of the ferry, inevitably has come the passing of some of the individuality and separateness which the near insularity of the place imparted. Journey times to work have been greatly cut, and the Black Isle has become, to many, a more desirable place in which to live. The construction of the improved communications network gave to Tore, a loose collection of houses, the distinction of being the most accessible settlement in the Black Isle, with roads converging on its giant roundabout from all directions.

Paradoxically, improved road links have resulted in the breaking of one long-established social link. In the past, Dingwall, the county town of Ross, was the obvious place to go for shopping and essential services. Now, loyalties have shifted. Inverness has become the popular service centre for a great proportion of the Black Isle population. There can be no denying the many advantages which the bridging of the firths has brought. At the same time, it would be a pity if that distinctiveness which has always been the hallmark of the Black Isle were to be greatly reduced as a result.

CHAPTER 11

Avoch and the Fishing

For the passing visitor, the little fishing village of Avoch offers more than just a pleasant stopping point on the through road to Cromarty. The harbour and nearby huddle of fisher cottages are an obvious reminder of the important part once played by the fishing in the life of the community, but there is also a rich, unseen story to be told of the village and its folk.

But beware a pitfall! The spelling of the village name is strangely at odds with local pronunciation. The origin of the name would seem to be a Gaelic description of the geographical situation of the place, namely from Abhach, the river-place.

The earliest seatown settlement lay on the flat land near the mouth of the Goose Burn which drains the parish farmlands. The confused layout of old cottages known as the Dock represents some of the earliest fisher housing, and is best discovered on foot, for its creators certainly did not have the needs of the motor car in mind. Since the low cottages abut directly on to very narrow streets, householders have taken the precaution of positioning large stones at the corners to fend off over-close vehicles.

The small parallel streets (locally known as 'the streeties') which run from the High Street to the sea bear the family names (John Street, James Street, George Street, Margaret Street) of the Mackenzie lairds of Avoch. Just across the burn mouth, lies another row of low, white-walled fisher cottages, also the laird's creation, and so, in a limited way at least, Avoch may be placed among the ranks of the northern planned villages.

The mainstay of Avoch was always the fishing. Originally, the firth in front of the village provided much of its living. Herring, notorious for their unpredictability, nevertheless appeared regularly enough to provide the important winter fishing known as the 'kessacks' or Kessock herring. Sprats similarly shoaled in enormous quantities within the confines of the firth, and this 'garvie' fishing was also an important feature

In the old days, the small fishing boats were drawn up all along the sea front at Avoch. Though it retains the flavour of a fishing village, fishing no longer dominates the occupations of its folk.

of the village's seasonal round.

With life lived at a subsistence level, families had little to come and go on. It was the kind of situation where crises might always lurk around the corner, and the *Ross-shire Journal* of April 1883 notes that the Avoch minister had received a gift of money to be distributed among the most destitute of village families 'following the almost complete recent failure of the herring and garvie fishing'.

In the early decades of the present century, the pattern of the fishing was markedly different from that of today. The smallest boats were the 'skufteys' which were used close to shore, often by the older men. They were also a useful means of ferrying back and fore people and goods to larger boats lying offshore. A combination of Black Isle larch and local skill produced the clinker-built 'scaffies'. A brown lug sail completed the picture of a finely proportioned craft that was for long the mainstay of the fleet. As Peter Anson remarked of Avoch in his classic account of the east coast fishing, 'There are few fishermen today who would venture in a small boat all the way from the upper end of the Moray Firth to the coast of Northumberland and back, with neither chart nor compass, nor any knowledge of navigation'. Yet some of the Avoch men did just that in days long gone, and won admiration around the coast for their achievement.

At the end of the winter herring fishing, the round-stemmed scaffies were hauled up out of the water, and sometimes right into the burn mouth. The long summer days would find the little boats fishing away from their home port, along the north coast in Caithness, or over in the west around Loch Broom.

But the need to pursue the herring far from shore called for a vessel more robust than the open scaffie. The 'Zulu', which was first introduced just across the Moray Firth, commemorated in its name the South African Zulu Wars, and alongside some 'Fifies' became the mainstay of the fleet.

Avoch was to continue with its scaffies for long afterwards, though the bigger wooden vessels opened up new possibilities for the summer fishing which followed the migrating shoals from Shetland down to Caithness and Buchan, then further south again to the great English herring meccas of Lowestoft and Yarmouth. Following the fishing went the Avoch fisher lassies, some of them no more than fourteen years old, with their wooden 'kistacks', filled with their most necessary possessions. When the fishing was at its peak, the young women gutted and packed the herrings into wooden barrels, their fingers tightly bound with 'clooties' to give some protection against cuts and stinging brine.

Apart from net fishing, there was also some setting of cod nets around Tarbat Ness in Easter Ross and of baited lines for white fish in the same area. Working at the lines took place mainly between the winter and summer fishings, and involved enormous effort. First the bait had to be gathered, involving a sail or tramp round to Munlochy Bay. Mussels and lug worms were then gathered and transported back to the village by skuftey or creel. Mussels not immediately required were then stored in the 'larachs', simple stone enclosures in front of the village. When required, the live mussels were then laboriously shelled and the baited hooks carefully arranged in a flat container called a 'skoo'.

The life of the Avoch fishermen was certainly a challenging

one in the days of the old sailing craft. Down in the bowels of the boats, the bread was sometimes suspended in baskets to guard against the unwelcome attention of the rats with whom the fishermen shared their life at sea. Latterly, the sweat of hoisting mast and sail was reduced by the installation of steam boilers' on the old sailing craft, though their motive power remained the wind.

Neither did the fishermen enjoy the benefits of modern technology to locate the shoals. Instead of studying sonar signals, they were practiced in the art of reading nature's signs. The presence of spouting whales was noted with more than passing interest. Concentrations of 'maas' (gulls) were useful indicators of the presence of shoals, as were diving 'solan geese' (gannets). However, an important distinction was made between the adult and immature forms of the latter.

The dark-plumaged (and therefore inexperienced) young 'black solans' were considered unreliable, but the large white adults with their distinctive black wing tips were good indicators as they plummetted like darts into the sea around the boats. Indeed, the manner of their diving was also useful, and an experienced fisherman could use it to distinguish between different fish species. More conclusive evidence was obtained from solans which were so full of fish that they were unable to rise from the water. At the approach of a boat, the sated solans would regurgitate a large part of their heavy meal to assist in take-off, and then the fishermen could tell for sure what they had been feeding on.

Not surprisingly, the fishermen had their own names for the birds with whom they shared the sea's largesse. Young gulls in juvenile plumage were 'grey allens' and black-headed gulls 'spekies'. Fulmars, because of their ancestral association with the remote islands to the west, were 'St Kildas' and their close relations, the little black storm petrels which flitted over the wave-tops, were 'oiley birdeys' because of their fondness for taking blobs of fish oil from the water round the boat.

The names of the old boats were as colourful as the speech of the men who crewed them. They ranged from the Biblical, as in the *Mizpah*, to the local such as the *Craig Wood*, and to the more exotic-sounding *Begonia* and *Bird of Freedom*. Sailing boats continued to work out of Avoch long after they ceased to operate from the other Moray Firth ports. The last sailing craft, the *Violet M. Hope* and the *Mizpah* still worked out of the port until the late 1920s. At the end of her Avoch days the latter went westwards to Stornoway, the last place on the Scottish coast to use these old sail-powered fishing boats.

In 1988, Mr Alexander MacLeman recalled for the writer his days on the brown-sailed vessels. As a youthful cook on the *Violet M. Hope*, it was his job to prepare the meals for the crew, using the stores which each had separately brought aboard. When working out of western places like Barra, food was often far from fresh, but an outbreak of blue mould among the bread, which would consign the whole loaf to the waste bin today, was simply scraped away.

Meat was brought aboard in the form of cured legs of ham, and Mr MacLeman could recall the problems of slicing the tough meat, having on occasion had to rely secretly on his father's prized cut-throat razor to make any impression. Pipe smoking was the norm among the men, and when stores were carried out to the boats they would include parcels of no less than seven pounds of tarry, black Bogie Roll XXX, a strong tobacco that filled the area below decks with a powerful aroma and lingering blue reek.

Apart from local demand, a combination of fish, potatoes and oatmeal being the staple diet of the fisher folk, the landings from the Avoch boats found a ready market up the firth at Inverness. It was the job of the women to supply fish to the farms and cottages of the rural hinterland, tramping the many side roads with heavy creels laden with fish on the outward journey and with bartered farm produce on their return. This was a regular point of contact between the fishing and farming communities of the Black Isle who seemed otherwise to have little in common.

Yet there were strong similarities. Both lived a life little removed above a subsistence level, and the daily doings of both were equally bound up with the vagaries of weather. Another contact between the two cultures came at the annual threshing time on nearby farms, when the women would go to the farmyards where the threshing 'millacks' were working and there fill their sacks with 'caff' (grain chaff) to stuff the family bedding in days when sprung mattresses were unknown.

George Street, Avoch — one of the parallel 'streeties' running down from the High Street to the shore. In the background, the spire of the parish kirk rises among the trees.

If their menfolk lived with the unpredictability of the sea, then the women of Avoch frequently lived with the uncertainties of family life in days when things were at such a basic level. Even into this century, there was more than a passing resemblance in their lifestyle to that of the women in today's developing world, now so familiar on our television screens. The tedious and time-consuming chores of water carrying and firewood gathering were two obvious parallels.

Water was obtained from communal pumps strategically positioned along the village streets, but slopping water pails had to be laboriously carted back to the houses. Firewood was gathered in the well-wooded environs of the village, though not necessarily with the blessing of the high-handed managers of the land. Enormous 'burdeens' of twigs and branches were carried back under bowed backs to keep the fire going in grates where fish and 'tatas' (potatoes) were boiled. In addition to all this, it was the duty of the women to wade out to the fishing boats, carrying their menfolk on well-strengthened backs so that they could start their fishing trips dryshod.

Even today, the story is told in Avoch of a woman known as Katie Gak whose job it was to take passengers to and fro in a skuftey to the little steamer offshore. Those disembarking from the boat were rowed to shore, then transported to the beach on Katie's strong back. On one occasion, she had the task of giving a 'piggy back' to the very same estate keeper who had previously chased her from the nearby woods for firewood gathering. On the way from skuftey to shore, the otherwise sure-footed Katie just happened to stumble, immersing her human burdeen in the sea. Though the memory of so many of those hardy women of old Avoch has gone with the passing of the generations, that of Katie Gak lives on, for the local laird had her portrait painted, and any visitor transacting financial business can still see it hanging in the local office of the Bank of Scotland.

In time, the bigger ports along the Moray coast and on the North-east knuckle began to forge ahead with their large fleets of steam drifters. Lossiemouth, Macduff, Fraserburgh and Peterhead emerged as main centres of the fishing industry, while many of the smaller northern villages with difficult harbours began to languish. But while nearby Cromarty eventually failed altogether as a fishing centre, Avoch continued, a fact due less to the quality of its harbour than to the acumen of the men who sailed from it.

The Avoch community was close-knit by character and close-bound by family ties. A comparatively small number of surnames existed within the village. The primary school roll in the 1950s showed that one third of the one hundred and thirty pupils bore the characteristic Avoch surnames of Patience, Jack and MacLeman. In such circumstances, by-names were an absolute necessity to avoid confusion. The Avoch list is staggering in its variety, ranging from Cyich to Kyunduck, Meyrican to Moochel.

An incomer in the old days could never hope to master the complexity of the by-name structure, nor the intricacies of pronunciation of village speech. The archaic use of 'thees' and 'thous' is only one of the obvious differences between the speech of Avoch and the rest of the Black Isle. Another is the dropping of the initial aspirate, a horse, for example, being 'a 'orse'.

The commonly addressed rhetorical question 'How should I know?' is rendered 'Aar duv I ken?' The 'ey' sound at the end of words, as in 'birdey', sounds vaguely Norse in its 'Auchie' pronunciation. Much has been said about the supposedly unique nature of the vocabulary. The fact is that it is often the pronunciation alone that is unique, many of the words being identifiably Scots or Gaelic when closely examined. Nevertheless, in its old form the native speech was a colourful language, not least in its use of expletives such as 'Deevell stench thee!' But that was pretty strong stuff. The much more moderate, 'O, vowv the day!' is still a commonly used exclamation.

Avoch speech is also liberally laced with diminutives, a boy, for example, being a 'sheelee' (North-east 'chiel') or 'sheelakee' and a girl a 'deymak' or 'deymakee'. To use the example of the horse again, this might just as commonly be 'a orsack' or even 'a orsakey', depending on the size of the horse or the age of the person being addressed. At times, the language could be used in the most economical way, a good example being the still commonly used greeting 'Ut now?' which defies exact translation.

In the late 1920s, there were still well over two hundred village fishermen, though the writing was on the wall for their old sailing craft, for there were already many motor-powered boats in the local fleet. When the old stalwarts were retired elsewhere, the Avoch scaffies continued to find a role in the winter sprat fishery up the firth. But the days of scaffie and Zulu were numbered, as the new boats took over. All that remains today as a reminder of the days of sail are some fading photographs and a few blackened Zulu ribs sticking out of the Munlochy Bay silt, for this was a traditional last resting place for the old boats when all useful pieces had been stripped from them.

The inter-war years were difficult ones for the village. The Rev. David Sutherland who knew the village in the old days has done a service to northern social history by recalling life in Avoch between the wars in his little book 'Fisherlore of Avoch'. In it, he describes the strong community spirit which rose above the material poverty of the age.

For generations, village life was lived in the shadow of the big house at nearby Rosehaugh. Originally the estate of Sir George Mackenzie, the 'Bluidy Mackenzie', Rosehaugh was to pass to the Fletcher family in 1864. The Fletchers' wealth derived from the profits of colonial plantations, and was channelled into a land acquisition that made the estate the most important by far in the Black Isle. In 1884, James Douglas Fletcher succeeded his father and wasted no time in creating one of the most lavish estate complexes in the north. At the end of last century, the existing house was greatly extended into a chateau-like sandstone extravaganza.

The surrounding gardens were just as impressive. Old maps recall the position of the race-course, the lakes with their boat-houses, the hydro-electric plant, and even the site of an eagle's aviary. The estate laundry and dairy were styled on the lines of the mansion house itself. The big house, its glittering balls and society ongoings were a constant source of wonder to the inhabitants of the village down the road, but it all generated employment in domestic and estate work.

The opulence of the big house was all the more impressive when set beside the material poverty of the village. Sanitation was of the most basic kind along the streets, and disease was endemic. The laird's response was to institute a village cleansing system. As at other fishing harbours around the coast, however, the fisherman often resorted to a privy overhanging the water beside the burn, relying on the natural flushing mechanism beneath. David Sutherland recalls how mischievous village boys used to place themselves in a strategic position below for aiming their catapults with accuracy at the posteriors of the occupants therein.

Today, the Avoch fishing fleet is much slimmed down from the old days. For a time, the sleek, varnished brown boats of the Avoch men with rows of hanging black tyres along their sides were a familiar sight in West Coast ports with their INS registrations. But now those ring net boats have also faded from the fisheries scene. The summer visitor to Avoch might be forgiven for thinking that the fishing industry has died altogether, for there are seldom any of the bigger boats to be seen in the tidal harbour. This is due to the fact that the boats work away from home, their crews travelling by minibus to West Coast ports such as Ullapool and Mallaig.

Mrs Betty Jack of Avoch, pictured in the family net shed in 1942 where she is engaged in shelling mussels for the fishing lines. (Photograph courtesy of her grand-daughter, Mrs Margaret Campbell, Ullapool).

The fishermen themselves have largely forsaken the old seatown where their ancestors lived in the huddle of thatched cottages, preferring instead the more spacious modern housing above the village.

Today, the old fisher cottages have been considerably improved, but with their modernisation has come change. The proportion of village families now dependent on the fishing has greatly decreased, and incomers who know little of the old Avoch ways and speech form a steadily increasing proportion of the population.

Inevitably, the distinctive speech is under threat. Pupils in the school mix daily with the children of recent local incomers and those brought by bus from neighbouring Fortrose and Rosemarkie. In the face of such cosmopolitan linguistic pressure, the local speech is failing to perpetuate itself among the new generations. And the process of decline is further hastened by the transfer of all Avoch pupils to Fortrose Academy for their secondary education.

As elsewhere in Scotland, where the true speech of the folk suffered from misguided attempts to replace it with 'proper' English, the Avoch tongue was regarded with some contempt by the educational and ecclesiastical establishment. For example, writing the parish account in the Third Statistical Account of Scotland, the Avoch minister noted in 1954 that 'Persevering attack over a long period on the more uncouth local pronunciations has led to a marked diminution in their use and pupils leaving school today express themselves as well as most'.

The richly flavoured language of old Avoch was essentially the language of the fisher community. It was perpetuated in a particular style of life and in the shared experience of a close-knit community.

Though the horizons of many within that community were broadened considerably more than those of their farming neighbours by their travels after the herring shoals, the community was nevertheless insular to a degree which perpetuated the richness of its speech. That insularity is in large measure now passing, and with it the language of the old folk slips slowly away.

A few of the old traditions survive, however. A village wedding is still marked by the hoisting of flags. At the church door, the appearance of the newly weds is accompanied by a 'scrammie', an undignified scrabble to pick up as many as possible of the coins tossed into the air by the groom.

Although the importance of the fishing as a source of income may have declined overall, Avoch still retains the character of a fishing village. The local boats hardly use the harbour at all these days, but it is still somehow the focus of the village, and fine summer days bring the retired fishermen out to pass comment on the comings and goings of the small pleasure craft which now use it. In recent times, an offshore fish farm has been established in front of the village, rearing expensively produced salmon for southern markets, a far cry from the herrings once sold for a few pence by the women with their creels.

Apart from an income from the remaining fishing boats and for employment generated in local services, Avoch has now become more of a base for commuters to Inverness and round about than the focus of a local economy. But of the old days when fishing dominated village life, there are plenty of reminders, and the visitor can spend a pleasant hour or so seeking out the past in this Black Isle settlement of rich character.

CHAPTER 12

Rosemarkie and Fortrose

Rosemarkie is both the name of a Black Isle parish and of its firth-side village. The place-name has varied down through the years, appearing as Rosemarkyn on the old burgh seal, and as Rosemarky in quite recent times. Watson, in his *Place Names of Ross & Cromarty*, gives the origin as the Point of the Horse Burn, from the Gaelic ros meaning a point and maircnidh, possibly deriving from marc, a horse. Certainly, local pronunciation until recent times has rendered the village name 'Rosemarkney'.

Whatever the origin of its name, the visitor can discover here a settlement of character and charm. The early advantages of the village site are immediately apparent. Flat land which could be easily cultivated fronted a bay where fish might be caught or shellfish gathered. The Horse Burn, was an unfailing source of water, and the hill behind gave protection from biting north winds. In this pleasant corner of the Black Isle, village life was to flourish for centuries.

In time, church and community life were to become strongly linked as a wave of Christian mission from the west broke on a heathen Black Isle shore. St Moluag's early Christian settlement followed in the tradition of the missionaries of the Celtic Church who carried the Gospel from the islands of Lismore and Iona by way of the western seaways and across to the east coast. St Moluag of Lismore is said to have been buried at Rosemarkie at the end of the sixth century. In the early eighth century, the name of St Boniface (Curitan) begins to appear in the historical record, and he is said to have reorganised the settlement which the saintly Moluag had established, dedicating it to St Peter.

Rosemarkie's connection with the Pictish world has already been mentioned. By the twelfth century, the ecclesiastical importance of this corner of the Black Isle had been confirmed by its establishment as centre of the See of Ross. By the following century, the small cathedral chapter was enlarged, and it is considered that this may mark the time of the transfer

Chanonry Ness, once famed for its salmon fishing (note the ice-houses in the background), is now best known for its eighteen-hole golf course.

of its centre to Fortrose. On a flat site, close to water supplies and with a commanding view across the firth, the great sandstone cathedral was erected to the glory of God and to the credit of the squad of skilled masons who shaped the stones and fitted them into place.

Though an independent burgh, Rosemarkie was to live somewhat in the shadow of the flourishing cathedral settlement a short distance away. In 1661, by Act of Parliament, Rosemarkie was united with Fortrose. But being administratively joined to its more powerful neighbour up the road certainly did not mean that Rosemarkie was going to surrender its individuality, and the village continued as a centre of Black Isle rural life.

Indeed, village life in the early nineteenth century was just the lastest stage in the slow evolution of a pattern established centuries before. The folk cultivated the land and fished the firth, and provided services for themselves and for those in the countryside round about. In 1821, there were 314 village residents, half of the Fortrose total.

At that time, the parish kirk continued as centre of village life. The Rev. Alexander Wood noted of his flock that 'The people in the parish are, generally speaking, sober, cleanly and industrious; and appear in every respect contented with their condition, and the circumstance in which Divine Providence

121

has been pleased to place them'. However, he was anxious that the number of 'low tippling houses' be reduced.

In the days before improved communications put Rosemarkie within easy access of Dingwall and Inverness, the local tradesmen and craftsmen had an important role in the fabric of community life. The shoemaker kept the folk shod. The tailor, untroubled by the fickleness of changing fashion, produced clothing that was serviceable and designed to last. The cartwright made and repaired the wheels of communication. The mason built homes for the living and prepared memorials to the dead, and to a background of creaking water-wheel, the miller turned oats into meal in his mill beside the burn.

Crops were largely cultivated for human consumption, but some were for manufacture. The modern practice of producing large amounts of fodder crops for livestock was then undeveloped. Flax was grown in fields round about and steeped in a series of ponds called 'the pows' which obtained water from the mill lade. Their remains may still be seen today in front of the house in the Fairy Glen. In later years, they were also a source of winter ice for storage in the salmon fishers' ice-houses. Flax was also steeped in the Manse Loch just outside the village, but the practice offended the minister's nose in his grand manse across the road and it was later drained at his own expense.

Deft village hands converted the lint into hard-wearing linen cloth in an era when self-sufficiency was the hallmark of rural community life. Little of the old linen has survived, though at the yearly communion service in the village kirk, a few examples of hard-wearing Rosemarkie linen pew cloths continue in use.

Boatbuilding was another local trade last century. From a yard on the sea front, quite substantial craft were launched into the firth. Best known of these is perhaps the *Louisa,* named after Mrs Louisa Fowler of Raddery in 1852, and said to have been constructed out of larch from the Raddery woods.

But the old order, established and accepted over so many Rosemarkie generations, was set to change. The laying of the railway line to Fortrose and the development of road transport improved the communications network and helped release the village from the thirlage of self-sufficiency. But in so doing, it began also to remove the need for those occupations which had for so long provided work for skilled hands.

The water wheel of the mill at the burn mouth briefly found a new use as an ingenious washing machine when soldiers were billetted in their hundreds across the water at Fort George during the First World War. Huge quantities of blankets were ferried across the firth to be laundered.

The agricultural engineer's workshop just outside the village serves the needs of the farming community today, but the smiddy's fiery anvil sparks and pungent aroma of singeing horse hooves have long since given way to the blue flame of welding torch and smell of diesel oil. Changing diet and more centralised production methods for manufacturing oatmeal have silenced the water wheel and rendered the meal mill redundant. The old mill dam and sections of the lade survive a short distance up the burn, and the grinding stones may be seen in the garden of the house which was converted out of the old building.

The old village tradesfolk have vanished, and with them the inherited skills of their forefathers. With the closure of the village primary school, Rosemarkie children left the village each day to be educated in Fortrose. On the death of its last parish minister in 1967, the Church of Scotland congregation of the old parish kirk at Rosemarkie was united with the neighbouring congregation of Fortrose, and yet another link with the past was broken.

Because of its fine sandy shore, backed by attractive rocks and trees, Rosemarkie has always had a particular summer appeal. At the end of last century, a small mansion house known as *Hawkhill* became a hotel, and successive additions have created the imposing Marine Hotel which now dominates the Rosemarkie sea front. Looking after the needs of paying guests was also a lucrative summer occupation for many homes in the village.

The days of the old residential seaside holiday may now have gone, but the appeal of the sandy beach is undiminished. Before completion of the Kessock Bridge, visitor pressure on Rosemarkie on a fine summer weekend was limited by the capacity of the ferry boat and by the early close of its Sunday service. But now Rosemarkie has become a weekend mecca for Inverness and round about in an area where sandy beaches are a scarce resource. The result, on a fine summer day, is the familiar 'honeypot' situation of parking problems, litter and environmental pressure.

The golf course on Chanonry Ness is an important local amenity, drawing visitors from a wide area. The golf club itself was established in 1888, but there is evidence that the game was being played by gentlemen on the links at the beginning of the previous century.

Away from the beach, Rosemarkie High Street bears the signs of shop closures. Only the basic services now remain, of vital importance to the old, but often by-passed by the young in favour of the greater range of services on offer in Inverness. It is the all too-familiar story of rural life in the late twentieth century.

A welcome recent development has been the establishment of Groam House Museum in an old building on the High Street. A strong feature of the museum is now the interpretation of the area's Pictish past. The most important exhibit is the famous Rosemarkie symbol stone, now spared further weathering by being housed indoors. It was formerly bound together by a hideous iron corset and stood outside the parish kirk. After a brief sojourn over the Fort George where it was skilfully repaired by the masons there, it was returned to its present place, though not before the floor was thoroughly reinforced to take its enormous weight.

Rosemarkie has clearly had an interesting past, but in more recent times, Fortrose has gained in stature at the expense of its smaller neighbour. Though long joined in burghal wedlock, the two communities always maintained a fierce independence of one another. There may, however, be a close relationship in their name elements. Watson considered the strong local accent on the first syllable of Fortrose to be adjectival, derived from fo, under. As in Rosemarkie, he suggested that the latter part might be from ros, a promontory. There has been an increasing tendency on the part of incomers to mis-pronounce the name, wrongly placing the stress on the last part, as in Montrose. There is certainly no truth in the suggestion that the name matches that of Fort George across the narrows of the firth.

Miss Elizabeth Mann, ballad monger, St Boniface Fair. Each year, the old fair is re-enacted in the shadow of the cathedral at Fortrose.

In the past, the whole area around the cathedral was known as the Chanonry of Ross, hence the name of the peninsula. This name also became corrupted into various forms. As the name of the settlement it is now obsolete, though there has been one survival of it. The older generation of Avoch folk refer to Fortrose as 'Shendrey', thereby perpetuating the old name and recalling the rival settlement's finest hour.

The establishment of the cathedral was to confer on Fortrose a status above all other Black Isle communities. Its importance as a centre of northern ecclesiastical life was reflected in the whole early lay-out of the settlement, with the manses of the priests grouped around the cathedral grounds. Each manse took the name of the parish served by members of the cathedral clergy. For example, the Manses of Contin and

Kiltearn stood near modern Union Street, and it is said that pieces of stonework from the old manse were incorporated into the front of the large house called St Katherine's. The Manse of Cullicudden and the Manse of Lemlair stood somewhere near the present day St Andrew's Church.

It is a great pity that the old surrounding buildings of the cathedral precincts have been replaced by today's housing, but the arched building at Rose Court is a fine survival from the past. This was the site of the pre-Reformation Deanery, Rosemarkie Manse, residence of the Dean of Ross.

There is a popular local tradition of a network of subterranean passageways beneath the cathedral and its precincts. In the past, local folk had a dread of one particular spot close to the cathedral and were loath to go near it or disturb it in any way for fear of unleashing a plague. This belief seems to have originated in an old tradition that the cathedral clergy had buried at that place a white sheet containing a virulent pestilence which they had somehow got hold of and exorcised with bell, book and candle. Whatever the origin of that story, the same area once yielded up a huge hoard of ancient Scots coins.

Street names confirm the Chanonry's past, including Dean's Road, Precints Road, Bishops Road and Palace Gardens near the site where the Bishop's Palace once stood. Below the cliff, beside Craig an Ron, the Seal's Rock, there is a deep hole which sometimes harbours a lobster. No doubt the Lord Bishop dined well in those early times, for the hole is known locally as the Bishop's Pot.

Its importance thus confirmed, Fortrose continued to function as the central place for the Black Isle long after the Chanonry clergy had gone and their grand cathedral had tumbled into ruin after them. The old stone market cross, though suffering the neglect of passing time and the company of some unlovely bollards, stands on a corner of the High Street as symbol of the burgh's former market function.

For a time, the town also had an industrial base. Before the mid-eighteenth century, the textile industry, based on locally grown flax, had a strong northern centre in Fortrose from which coarse linen was supplied to much of northern Scotland. The increasing importance of the activity in a number of other

Alexander Alexander, master baker and former provost of the burgh, here pictured at his old Scots oven in Fortrose before he retired in 1984.

centres, such as Cromarty and Tain, gradually reduced its importance to Fortrose, however, and the role of the town tended to be as market and service centre for the surrounding part of the Black Isle. Industrial employment was available only on the smallest of scales, as in the long defunct lemonade bottling factory. Its stoneware bottles have now become local collectors' pieces.

Until Government regionalisation policy removed the old Scottish burgh administrations in 1975, a town council managed the municipal affairs of both Fortrose and Rosemarkie. From an imposing Georgian-style Town House overlooking the cathedral chapter house where the town fathers had earlier met, weightly local matters ranging from road repairs to refuse removal were discussed.

A redundant church building in Rotten Row has assumed the role of town hall, where indoor bowlers now test their skill under the gaze of many stern-faced characters from the area's past. The fine portraits of the Seaforth Earls and their fair-skinned ladies which line the walls were the gift, in 1952, of Madeleine, Countess of Middleton to the burgh and its folk.

The Countess's Mackenzie ancestors were the Lords of Kintail, Earls of Seaforth and Chiefs of the Clan Mackenzie until the male line came to an end in 1815.

The Mackenzies had a long association with Chanonry since the sixteenth century when they appear to have acquired the Fortrose Castle and its lands from the Bishop of Ross. Indeed, the second earl was provost of the burgh. Among the nine splendid portraits are those of George's son Kenneth (Coinneach Mhor or Big Kenny), third Earl and Sherriff of Ross, who died in 1678, and of his wife the Countess Isabella. She was the granddaughter of Sir John Mackenzie of Tarbat, The Tutor of Kintail. She is depicted in her portrait as a well-bosomed, cold-looking character, and, rightly or wrongly, now has the reputation of having ordered the grisly burning of the Brahan Seer at Chanonry Point.

Until recent times, however, the Seaforth portraits were totally eclipsed by the enormous Benjamin West painting 'The Death of a Stag', depicting 'Alexander III of Scotland rescued from the fury of a stag by the intrepid Colin Fitzgerald'. The latter was a progenitor of the Clan Mackenzie. This painting of his heroic endeavour scene (possibly the largest painting in Scotland at over twelve by seventeen feet) completely filled the far end of the town hall. It had hung there since its removal from Brahan castle, prior to its demolition in 1952.

After its removal from Fortrose, the magnificent painting was saved from export across the Atlantic. After being purchased for over half-a-million pounds, it is now an important exhibit in the National Gallery in Edinburgh. Though the original has now gone, a smaller-scale coloured reproduction is on local display.

In addition to its ecclesiastical importance, Fortrose has long been noted as a centre of education. The present Academy, established in 1791, carried on the earlier tradition of the burgh grammar school. Indeed, the torch of learning had long burned in the Chanonry, though not without the occasional flicker. For example, in 1743 the Presbytery of Chanonry felt moved to castigate the schoolmaster for Sabbath breaking, drinking, gaming and for using profane language – a formidable indictment against one entrusted with the moulding of young minds. And there was more to come. An ardent supporter of Bonnie Prince Charlie, the schoolmaster had encouraged the boys to share his enthusiasm for the Jacobite cause during the '45 rebellion. He was accused of several instances of disloyalty, such as encouraging the boys to build a bonfire in honour of the pretender, and writing into their copy books 'Honour to Prince Charlie'.

The establishment of the new Fortrose Academy, with its teaching rector and two masters, gave an opportunity to present a broadened curriculum and put Fortrose in the very vanguard of education in the north. English language and grammar, Latin, algebra and trigonometry, arithmetic, geography and French were important subjects in the new curriculum, but it also encompassed astronomy and the elements of fortification and gunnery.

The teaching day began at 7 o'clock on summer mornings and at 8 o'clock in the winter, with a break for breakfast after a couple of hours of lessons. Notwithstanding the early start, there was also a night school, the third master being allowed to use his schoolroom for this purpose 'during the half-year from the Autumnal to the Vernal Equinox, for instructing such apprentice-lads, servants and mechanics in Fortrose or the neighbourhood'.

Subscriptions for the foundation of the new school poured in from as far afield as India and the West Indies, and an excellent educational reputation was soon established. Within nine years of the Academy's opening, however, yet another cloud hung over the character of the staff. In 1808, (the school records observing a discrete silence on the matter), the teaching staff had fallen foul of the Presbytery yet again, and apparently not without justification. Drunkenness and questionable ongoings with a serving maid were only a few of the charges levelled at all three of the masters in a scandal that must have given the burgh's gossips a field day.

One problem in attracting the right kind of staff was probably the poor level of salaries on offer. Out of their meagre earnings, each master was expected to provide annually for heating and lighting his classroom 'eight barrels of good English coals, two loads of good peats and eight pounds' worth of good candles'. Nothing but the best, it seems, would do for the Black Isle's foremost seat of learning. Small wonder,

Bridge Street, Rosemarkie. The old cottages nestle beneath the wooded face of the Red Craig, a great glacial deposit from which nesting fulmars cackle above the noise of traffic below.

then, that the rector and second master in 1812 raised the eyebrows of those who held the Academy's purse-strings by 'craving an immediate increase' of their salaries. This was greeted with the gravest suspicion by the school managers who were inclined to think that the request had been 'induced by the extravagant salaries lately announced to the teachers in the new academy at Tain'. The minor modifications at the school which followed shortly afterwards 'for enabling the rector and second master to rear a pig each if they please' were perhaps more of a necessity than a privilege.

With the closure of the junior secondary departments of the village schools, Fortrose Academy became the focus of all secondary education in the area. Through its wide range of courses (fortification and gunnery having long since been dropped from the curriculum), the school continues to maintain the high standards for which it has long been known throughout the Black Isle and beyond.

On summer days, large numbers of visitors descend from touring coaches to wander around the cathedral grounds, but many merely pass through on their way to Rosemarkie or Cromarty. An exception is the occasion of the St Boniface Fair, a revival of the medieval fair commemorating the Saint's feast

Roberto Pagliari, whose family have sold their home-made Italian ice cream to countless summer visitors to Rosemarkie beach.

day. For a whole afternoon in August, Cathedral Square is transformed into a bustling market place. Cars are banned, and wooden booths erected for the convenience of tradesfolk to display their wares. Black-gowned scrutineers inspect the booths to ensure the quality of the merchandise on offer. Ballad mongers recite appropriate verses, tumblers tumble and singers sing. All in all, it is a time of fun and enjoyment, but always at the mercy of the elements – hence the exhortation at the bottom of notices advertising the fair: 'Good people, pray for fine weather!'

Although the village (or city, as it should perhaps be called, by virtue of its cathedral status) stood to gain from the contraction of services in the surrounding settlements, the completion of the Kessock Bridge has now put the centre of Inverness within less than half an hour's driving time, and the consequences for existing local retail services are all too apparent.

Concern for fish stocks in the local rivers has recently led to the Atlantic Salmon Trust buying up the Chanonry Point fishings which had been worked for generations, testing the skills of the local fishers with their broad wooden cobles amid turmoil of currents and counter currents. A reminder of those past salmon fishings are the ice-houses at Chanonry Point and at Kincurdy, Rosemarkie, with their dark and dank interiors. Summer salmon fishing by net and coble continues along the Rosemarkie shore, trapping the fish as they nose their way upstream.

The Chanonry Point lightkeeper has gone, replaced by a technology that automatically lights the lantern and even switches to a backup beam should the main light fail. No longer do outgoing letters bear the post office frank 'Fortrose', a blow to local pride, and a further step towards centralisation. The village shoemaker has recently retired and no one has carried on his craft. When Alexander's High Street bakery closed in the spring of 1984, it was the ending of a link with past times when an unbroken succession of village bakers supplied the community with its daily bread, and at harvest time baked the beautifully crafted sheaf loaf which graced the kirk's thanksgiving service.

The widened horizons of the late twentieth century have undoubtedly conferred many advantages on Rosemarkie and Fortrose, but there must be some nostalgia and regret, too, in the knowledge that the old-established mould of Black Isle village life has been broken, and the old values of neighbourliness and community spirit are now less strong.

CHAPTER 13

Cromarty, County Town

MEANE WEIL, SPEAK WEIL, AND DO WEIL. So runs the motto on the seventeenth century Urquhart Stone from Cromarty Castle and on the old burgh arms. In the years that were to follow, Cromarty was to do very well indeed, assuming an unrivalled importance among the Black Isle settlements.

For many years, the town was administrative centre of the small county with which it shared its name. In reality, the county of Cromarty was a hopeless scatter of pieces of the Highlands placed together under one name and administration. This situation came about when Sir George Mackenzie of Tarbat was created first Earl of Cromartie in 1703. Of him Bishop Burnet is reported to have said that 'he had great notions of virtue and religion, but they were only notions'.

The fourteen separate pieces of his estates throughout Ross, stretching from the eastern Black Isle across to the West Coast with Ben Wyvis and Strathpeffer on the way, were then erected into the new county of Cromarty. This lasted until the Boundary Commissioners put an end to the inconvenient arrangement in the late nineteenth century.

Further administrative confusion resulted from much earlier times. In the fifteenth century, all the lands of the Thane of Cawdor, scattered throughout Ross, Nairn and Moray, were designated one thaneage. The result was that the Black Isle parish of Urquhart, in which most of the Thane of Cawdor's lands of Ross were located, was administered as part of Nairn-shire until 1891. As a consequence of this curious arrangement, the illicit distillers of Ferintosh who carried on their trade after the Government bought out the Ferintosh Privilege, used to be summoned to appear in the courthouse of Nairn, notwithstanding the fact that courts were held a few miles away at Dingwall and Cromarty.

The town of Cromarty had earlier been a burgh of barony, but that status had lapsed in the mid eighteenth century. It was then created a parliamentary burgh in 1833. With its past commercial importance based on a flourishing harbour trade, Cromarty was the Black Isle's commercial hub.

Cromarty's fortunes have always been closely tied to the firth over which it faces. Looking across to the farmlands of Easter Ross and the distant mountain backcloth, the small town seems almost to turn its back on the land of the Black Isle behind. In recent times, the settlement has paid the price of its geographical isolation at the furthest end of the peninsula, but in days gone by it enjoyed a reputation as one of the most flourishing towns of the Highlands. The surviving legacy of those more prosperous times is a great source of interest to the present day visitor keen to discover more of the fascination of this old Black Isle burgh.

As at Avoch, the fishermen of Cromarty exploited the fisheries of the adjacent firth and surrounding waters. As long as boats were small and catches limited, this renewable resource could be harvested fairly close to home. At times, the sea could be incredibly generous in its bounty, and around the time of the Union in 1707, the 'herring drove' was so plentiful that Cromarty curers were hard pressed to keep up with the supplies of fish being landed. Indeed, sometimes there was such a glut of fish that loads of herring were carted inland and spread on the farmlands as nitrogen-rich manure.

But just as at Avoch, the unpredictability of the herring shoals could spell economic and social ruin. Such a state of affairs was never more evident than in the early eighteenth century when Cromarty was hit by real depression. And if the sea could be grudging in its supply of natural resources, so could the land. The area was desperately short of fuel. Firewood was in short supply due to lack of tree planting in the past, and the local peat mosses were well nigh exhausted. Dried cow dung, much needed to coax the land into greater productivity, was instead burned in many a hearth, and the phrase 'A Cromarty fire' was uncharitably used to describe a fire that had gone out.

Fortunately, help was to hand in the person of a well-to-do merchant by the name of William Forsyth who recognised the commercial potential of the sheltered Black Isle harbour. Coastal trade was nothing new for Cromarty, but Forsyth possessed great business drive, and his sloops, the first of which

The old brewery, Cromarty. The once-flourishing port at the far end of the peninsula is rich in old buildings which are a reminder of the town's important past.

is said to have been built at Fortrose, along with the other vessels of the Cromarty fleet, plied a trade with east coast ports and across the North Sea. Cromarty thus came to enjoy the role of Highland entrepot, importing cargoes as diverse as timber from Norway, iron from Sweden, and delft ware and gin from Holland for distribution throughout the north. Much needed coal was imported from the north of England, and Cromarty had an important role in exporting Black Isle farm products.

As elsewhere in the Highlands, the seashore produced abundant seaweed resources hitherto used only as fertiliser for seaside fields. Forsyth now organised a local kelp trade, in which weed was gathered and cut before burning for its ash, a raw material much in demand by industry in the south. As northern agent of the British Linen Company, Forsyth also oversaw the development of spinning of imported flax and the manufacture of linen products. It was the beginning of a period of great prosperity for Cromarty, and the start of an industrial phase unparallelled in the north.

When the Cromarty estate was purchased by the wealthy

George Ross in 1772, its short term future prosperity was assured. As an admirer of William Forsyth, Ross was determined to build upon his predecessor's efforts, and, with government support, immediately put into effect the construction of a new pier that could accommodate large trading ships.

Manufacture of hemp rope and sailcloth became a major employer of labour in the town. Imported iron was converted to spades and nails, while instructors were brought north from England to initiate local women into the art of lace working. A substantial brewery was erected, as much to produce a more acceptable alternative to the widely consumed and potent local whisky as to manufacture a product for outside sale. Clearly, such a build-up of local manufacturing required a work force greater than the burgh, or indeed the Black Isle, could supply. George Ross's answer was to bring in families from the Highlands, families whose language was Gaelic, hence the Gaelic Chapel already mentioned.

But in the rapid rise of the smoky industrial towns of the south were sown the seeds of Cromarty's decline. Faced with competition from areas more favourably endowed with natural resources and linked together by a flourishing railway network, there was no way that a minor industrial centre in the north of Scotland could possibly compete.

In its trading heyday, the harbour had been the burgh's greatest asset. Now it lies largely disused. Part of the nearby rope works has been converted into local authority housing, thus ensuring the future of this fine red sandstone building from the past. The impressive three-storey brewery, after years of crumbling neglect, is to provide residential accommodation for a field study centre for art students from Robert Gordon's Institute of Technology in Aberdeen and Highland Regional Council.

A complementary future as studio and workshop is in store for the dilapidated Georgian stables and coach house of George Ross's striking Cromarty House, well hidden among its policy woodlands. In the long term, it is hoped that the natural, architectural and industrial environment of the town will draw visitors from other parts of the United Kingdom and beyond.

A short walk out of the village towards the South Sutor will take the visitor past one of the more bizarre features of the Black Isle. Anxious not to be troubled by the sight of servants and trades people coming and going from the big house, the laird of Cromarty had an enormous sandstone tunnel constructed so that their mundane comings and goings might not offend his gaze.

The elegant Forsyth House, with pillared entrance gate on the High Street, is a reminder of the man who set Cromarty on a firm commercial footing. At its eighteenth century economic peak, the town provided a model for Highland development that might well be the envy of those charged with present day planning. In fact, the thinking behind Cromarty's prosperity would surely have been appreciated by the Highlands and Islands Development Board, had that organisation been around in those days! The exploitation of local resources (including local labour), the use of communications facilities, and the fostering of new skills, underpinned by a plentiful flow of capital – these were the basis of Cromarty's eighteenth century 'economic miracle'. But in this case, the importance of individual business acumen cannot be overstated. It is good that so much remains to help piece together this important case-study of Highland economic development in the past. The visitor with a penchant for industrial archaeology will find much of interest in present day Cromarty.

The town was to continue as an important grain exporting port into the nineteenth century. The pork export trade begun by George Ross was greatly developed, again through the efforts of one individual, George Middleton, an Englishman who had come north to settle at Cromarty. Through his efforts, the port grew to be a major centre for trading in cured pork destined for the growing urban markets of the south.

The trading prosperity of the place was not destined to last beyond the middle of the century, however. Invergordon had long been drawing trade away across the firth. With its deep water and potentially larger hinterland, the Easter Ross port could mount a challenge which Cromarty proved unable to match. The result was a steady stagnation and decline throughout the rest of the nineteenth century. With the run down of its textile industry, and the uncertainties of its fishing, Cromarty's economic base had become firmly grounded in

F

trading. Inevitably, with the decline of its trading fortunes, the once prosperous town faced an uncertain future.

The present century brought its own unsettled times, and the monetary fortunes of war were to be spread in no small measure around the communities of the Cromarty Firth in two major world conflicts. The potential of the firth as a well-protected, deep-water naval base brought economic benefit to firthside communities at the same time as conflict robbed them of their men. The influx of servicemen meant a welcome boost to the local economy, and Cromarty came alive again with incomers, albeit temporary ones. The legacy of war may be noted in the remains of the heavy gun emplacements on the nearby Sutors. It may be seen also, and more poignantly, in the war graves within the town's graveyard beneath Hugh Miller's statue.

Some of the graves are of victims of the destruction of the cruiser HMS *Natal* on 30th December, 1915. At the time, a New Year's party was taking place on board. An invitation had gone out to local folk, but because it was a bad night for venturing out into the firth, many had chosen to stay at home. In the circumstances, it was a lucky escape, for sudden disaster was to come to those on board. In a fearful explosion that ripped the ship apart, no fewer than four hundred lives were lost. The official enquiry blamed the disaster on faulty cordite stowed away in the ship's munitions store, but local belief for years afterwards favoured a more colourful explanation involving spies and saboteurs.

The visitor on a day trip of discovery in the Black Isle should allow plenty of time to explore Cromarty. Hugh Miller's cottage has been a visitor attraction since the National Trust for Scotland took it over in the 1930s. Built by John Fiddes, a local pirate at the beginning of the eighteenth century, it was the birthplace in 1802 of the famous stonemason, geologist and writer. Two of the cottage's fascinating little rooms are furnished in the manner of Miller's lifetime, with low ceilings, wide chimney, baby's cradle and various kitchen plenishings. Upstairs, there is an attractively laid out small room with a display of fossils and rocks illustrating the geologist's local interests and research.

Hugh Miller's later days in Edinburgh as editor of *The*

Cromarty's Gaelic Chapel. Built to serve the needs of Gaelic-speaking workers brought in from the Highlands, the building is now roofless.

Witness newspaper are recalled in some large facsimile pages, and there is an informative audio-visual display on his life. Although so many of the old Cromarty buildings were once thatched, the whitewashed cottage is the only one to retain the old-style roofing. However, when a new roof was required, it was marsh reeds and English skills that were applied to create the present covering.

The narrow garden which runs up slope from Hugh Miller's cottage was probably once a kail yard, producing vegetables for the large black pot which hung on the open fire inside. Now it has been laid out with cottage garden plants as a colourful setting for the ornately carved sundial which flanks the deep well. Bearing the initials H M at its base, it was a gift from the young mason to his much loved uncles, James and Sandy.

Apart from Miller's birthplace, and the next door house built by his seafaring father (also restored by the National Trust for Scotland), there is no shortage of old sandstone buildings to be admired both for their architectural style and for their skilful use of local stone. Sometimes the red blocks are interlaced with pieces of black slate, adding further to the interest of their textue. A wander along the old streets and narrow vennels, past buildings with imposing frontages and corbie-stepped gable ends, is a journey into the past.

The elegant late eighteenth century courthouse with its domed cupola is a reminder of Cromarty's role as administrative town of the old county in past times. The copper-clad tower houses a clock specially made in Tain in 1782, and a bell which is much older. At the rear of the building the old jail remains in good order. The sixteenth century market cross was removed from its original site and placed in front of the courthouse. After years of disuse, the building has been renovated for a future role as burgh museum. The Hugh Miller Institute nearby, with is elaborately carved frontage, was a gift to the burgh from Andrew Carnegie and now houses the local library.

Cromarty lighthouse was built in 1846 by Alan Stevenson of the famous lighthouse designing family, and strongly resembles the one at Chanonry Point. Along from the lighthouse, the elegant primary school with its red sandstone tower was constructed thirty years later. Below the school stands a good example of a solidly constructed ice house, also with a Chanonry parallel.

To walk along The Paye, a narrow little road leading down into Church Street is to walk in the footsteps of the pilgrims of old who journeyed to the shrine of St Duthac at Tain. Following the route of the old highway, they came down into Cromarty along The Paye, en route for the ferry crossing to Nigg.

A much longer and more strenuous walk up the winding road to the South Sutor gives an excellent perspective on the town and its surrounding firth. Apart from the servant's tunnel at Cromarty House and the peaceful little graveyard of St Regulus, there are three eighteenth century houses on the edge of the town. Unfortunately, the fine L-plan house on the right hand side of the road is in a sad state of decay.

There is a strong tradition of an earlier settlement, now gone, on the lower ground. Whatever the true circumstances of its effacement from the map of today, there used to be plenty of stories told around winter firesides about the old lost village. Early last century there were said to be elderly residents who could remember the place before erosion by the sea had done its worst. For example, an old man claimed that he had been out in a boat half a century before with an elderly person who claimed that he 'was now guiding the helm where, sixty years before, he had guided the plough'.

There is no doubt that coastal erosion has been the means of destruction of East Coast settlements, but it is difficult now to be sure of the facts in Cromarty's case. Certainly, severe gales from the north-east are capable of lashing the coastline at that point, but so far the modern settlement has survived, despite the supposed prediction of Thomas the Rhymer that Cromarty would be twice destroyed by the sea.

High above the supposed site of the lost village of Cromarty, the top of the South Sutor is a reminder of the Cromarty Firth's key role in the country's defence in two world wars. This viewpoint gives an excellent panorama across the Moray Firth and far away to the hills of Ross and Sutherland. On a clear day, even the outline of the statue of the Duke of Sutherland on his hill-top plinth near Golspie may be distantly seen. In early summer, the calls of nesting kittiwakes carry across the water from the well-whitewashed seabird cliffs of the North Sutor.

This is also an excellent vantage point from which to view the oil platform construction yard at Nigg and the oil terminal from the Beatrice oilfield, closest to shore of all the North Sea fields. Crude oil travels by undersea pipeline from Beatrice to Nigg and is then removed by large tankers which tie up at the specially constructed deep-water jetty opposite the town.

After periods of prosperity, followed by days of economic decline, Cromarty has had to adjust to difficult circumstances. The town's comparative isolation puts it at a disadvantage relative to the other Black Isle settlements, especially Fortrose. Recent years have seen a steady decline in the range of local services, though some shops have found a new use. Increasingly, the old town is capitalising on the tourist trade, with several craft shops and tearooms where more basic retail services once existed. Long neglected buildings are being renovated and slowly the town is taking on a more lively air again. The pity is that so many of the local services have already gone. The introduction of the vehicle ferry to Nigg means that, to a limited extent at least, the town is no longer at the end of the road, though the advantage may be as much

G

psychological as economic.

To walk round old Cromarty is to meet with its prosperous past. Grand houses set back off the road contrast with low fisher cottages and the little vennels which connect them with the sea. Prophetically, perhaps, when they came to place the statue of Hugh Miller atop the great stone pillar in the middle of last century, he was set to look in the direction of the area where a modern generation of geologists found oil in ancient rock strata.

An amusing story is told concerning the statue. John Wilson, a school inspector at the turn of the century, was walking through Cromarty one day. In front of him was Hugh Miller, junior, who was also a geologist. As two boys came past, Wilson heard one say to the other: 'Ye see thon man, Tam? He's a son o' the moniment'.

North Sea oil has brought some prosperity to Cromarty, creating jobs in the platform construction yard across at Nigg, but for others with a less direct stake in the business, the industrial outlook across the narrows has not always been greeted with the same enthusiasm. Unfortunately, the platform construction business has seen its ups and downs. Large-scale employment has been followed by downturns which have decimated the work-force at the yard.

It is all too painfully obvious that Cromarty's economic history has been set in a 'boom and bust' kind of scenario. The rise and fall of the fishing; development and decline of the local industries; the build-up and run-down of the naval presence; the expansion and growth of the oil-related industry. Cromarty has seen them all, and its townsfolk have enjoyed the good times and the bad.

Cromarty's past loss may well prove to be its future gain. The economic decline that set in from the middle of last century, along with the changed pattern of communication, meant that, in geographical terms, the town was out on a limb. The result was a period characterised by stagnation and lack of change. In its way, the old town represents a kind of Scots burgh time-capsule with its crow-stepped gables and narrow lanes.

In these present times of increased leisure and greater mobility, it may be that Cromarty, so redolent of its colourful past, may come to be thankful that so much has remained to

Church Street, Cromarty. The cupola roof of the old burgh court house rises above the thatched roof of Hugh Miller's cottage.

recall those departed days. In an age of mass uniformity, a place as distinctively different as this must surely find a way to capitalise fully on this unique legacy from the past.

CHAPTER 14

Hugh Miller, Northern Naturalist

For many years Hugh Miller's cottage in Cromarty has been a place of pilgrimage for geologists and one of general interest to summer visitors. In the days before the A9 improvements, many an excursion into the Black Isle was prompted by the old National Trust sign between Beauly and Muir of Ord, pointing to the birth-place of the Black Isle's most celebrated son. Sadly, Miller seems to have been largely forgotten these days, yet his achievement was a remarkable one.

Between his origins in the humble Cromarty cottage and later literary status in Edinburgh as newspaper editor, Hugh Miller was to make an immense contribution to the emerging science of geology. Yet to state it in such terms is somehow to suggest an image of Miller as scientist, when he should perhaps be seen more as one of the great northern naturalists of the nineteenth century.

In the early decades, naturalists Robert Dick and Thomas Edward flanked Miller on either side of the Moray Firth, the one a baker in Thurso, the other a souter in Banff. More significantly, however, their pioneering work in natural history parallelled that of the Cromarty stonemason. Their achievement was born of a remarkable spirit of independent enquiry that was deeply rooted in the countryside around them.

For Robert Dick it was the plants and rocks of the Caithness countryside that lifted his horizons beyond the early morning tedium of the baking board. And whenever he was able, Thomas Edward left his last and stole away to the countryside to study the birds and beasts of the Banff and Buchan coast. But in a way which made him outshine both, the Cromarty mason's mind probed deeper than the surface of the sandstone which he shaped to ponder the very origins of the Black Isle rocks.

In the present age, when pocket field guides are available on all manner of countryside subjects, it is hard to imagine the identification problems those early naturalists must have faced.

Cromarty's most celebrated son. The sandstone figure of Hugh Miller looks beyond the paraphenalia of the oil-related industry towards the North Sea. Miller was one of the founding fathers of the science of geology which brought the North Sea oil industry into being.

Yet the most lavishly produced field guide is no substitute for the enquiring mind, so that a prodigious written communication was Miller's means of adding yet more pieces to the emerging pattern of the Black Isle's natural history.

Hugh Miller undoubtedly, owed much to his two uncles for his boyish interest in what would now be termed the environment. But wherever the original seeds of enquiry lay, the Cromarty boy's start as an apprentice stonemason was to be the means of bringing the Black Isle and its rocks to a world-wide readership. To a large extent, Miller's writings have been neglected in recent times, which is a pity, for they can add much to the enjoyment of discovering the Black Isle. Even today, generations after his untimely death in Edinburgh, enormous pleasure may be gained from following – even a little – in the footsteps of the Black Isle's most widely known son.

As a mason's apprentice, the young Hugh's practical introduction to local geology began in a freshly opened quarry overlooking the Cromarty Firth. Under the covering layer of boulder clay, a sandstone face was being exploited for building stone. It was tedious toil, and so a diverting interest in the living world was a great asset. Recalling the scene of his first working days long after the quarry had become overgrown, Miller writes of the place 'in which I first experienced the evils of hard labour, and first set myself to lessen their weight by becoming an observer of geological phenomena'.

In the manner of the old naturalists, Miller's interest was not based solely on one aspect of the environment. On that first apprentice day, gunpowder charges had been used to loosen the rock, and in the aftermath of one explosion the body of a goldfinch was found. Recalling the incident, Miller describes the beautiful bird, '. . . with its hood of vermilion, and its wings inlaid with the gold to which it owes its name'.

It is clear from his writings on those early days that there was an escape from the tedium of the job in contemplating the scenic panorama all around. 'Ben Wyvis rose to the west, white with the yet unwasted snows of winter, and as sharply defined in the clear atmosphere as if all its sunny slopes and blue retiring hollows had been chiselled in marble. A line of snow ran along the opposite hills: all above was white, and all below was purple.' Appropriately for a stonemason, he compares the Ben's glacial corries to sculpted marble, and this spectacular winter view is one that can be appreciated the more today by recalling that apt description.

Unfortunately for Miller's employer, but by great good luck for the aspiring young geologist, the quarry proved difficult to work and was abandoned in favour of another not far from the South Sutor of Cromarty. This move allowed an excursion into a totally different geological world, and even on the first day, Miller made an exciting new discovery. Smashing open a limestone nodule with his hammer, he revealed 'a beautifully finished piece of sculpture'. It was obviously some interesting fossil remain, but the apprentice's limited geological knowledge did not yet equip him for making a detailed identification. 'Of all Nature's riddles', he wrote, 'these seemed to me to be at once the most interesting and the most difficult to expound'.

Showing his exciting find to a fellow work-mate, Miller was told that there was 'a part of the shore about two miles farther to the west where curiously-shaped stones, somewhat like the heads of boarding-pikes, were occasionally picked up; and that in his father's day the country people called them thunderbolts, and deemed them of sovereign efficacy in curing bewitched cattle'.

The area referred to was the shoreline at Eathie, where the much younger Jurassic strata are faulted against the older rocks and exposed at low water. Miller lost no time in exploring the site, absorbed in his fascination for the multitude of fossils contained in the soft, sea-washed shale. It is a scene that has intrigued generations of visitors to the Eathie shore, for the beautifully coiled ammonites stand out in startling white contrast against the black mudstone in which they are entombed. Thrilled at this new find, Miller felt his imagination 'paralysed by an assemblage of wonders'. In time, he was to learn that the Eathie thunderbolts were really the fossilised hard parts of the extinct belemnites.

This really was a discovery to fire the imagination. 'My curiosity, once fully awakened, remained awake,' he recalled. But it was to be in the realms of the more ancient strata of the Old Red Sandstone that Miller was to make his greatest contribution to expanding geological knowledge. Familiar though he was with the appearance of the sandstone, he still lacked the knowledge of its wealth of fossil remains. He wrote: 'I was acquainted with the Old Red Sandstone of Ross and Cromarty for nearly ten years ere I had ascertained that it is richly fossiliferous'.

From our perspective in time, when the science of geology has revealed so much, it seems strange that such an important fact should have been so little known at the time. Indeed, the very existence of the Old Red Sandstone as a distinct geological formation had long been disputed. Sir Roderick Murchison, one of the greatest geologists of his age, told how he had been advised to give up its study, on the grounds that it was 'a mere local deposit, a doubtful accumulation huddled up in a corner'.

By a curious coincidence, Sir Roderick Murchison, who later

became President of the Royal Geographical Society, was also born in the Black Isle. His birthplace and family home was Tarradale House on the shores of the Beauly Firth near Muir of Ord. At the present time, the house serves as a field centre for Highland studies, administered by the Geography Department of the University of Aberdeen. Though his direct Black Isle connection was severed with the selling of the house, Murchison was to carry on an important written dialogue with Hugh Miller on various geological matters.

Once embarked on his study of the local sandstone, Miller made many important discoveries, one of the most fascinating being the presence of an intriguing fossil, the winged fish. This was to be named Pterichthys milleri by the famous Swiss geologist Agassiz in honour of its Black Isle finder. Miller could hardly contain his excitement on first opening the rock in which its outline had reposed unseen for millions of years. 'It opened with a single blow of the hammer; and there on a ground of light-coloured limestone, lay the effigy of a creature fashioned apparently out of jet, with a body covered with two plates, two powerful-looking arms articulated at the shoulders, a head as entirely lost in the trunk as that of the ray or the sun-fish, and a long angular tail. My first-formed idea regarding it was, that I had discovered a connecting link between the tortoise and the fish.' Some specimens of his exciting find were immediately dispatched to Murchison, but since the latter's researches were then more into the details of the Silurian system, they were passed to Agassiz for comment.

The Devonian era, in which the rocks of the Old Red Sandstone were deposited, was a time when vast numbers of fish must have crowded into evaporating shallows. In time, their packed remains were fossilised in the fish-beds which became Miller's happy hunting ground along the Cromarty shore, near the mouth of the Den of Eathie and along the Killen Burn. There were some strange and exciting finds among those early fish fossils. Some of the types which swam those ancient seas were armour-plated with tough scales. Some resembled the celebrated coelocanth, once thought extinct, but which made history by being rediscovered earlier this century in the depths of the Indian Ocean.

The Black Isle fish beds provided Miller with an opportunity to reconstruct the bodily form of long extinct fishes from a hotch-potch of fossil remains. It was exciting and frequently pioneering work, but there was a frustrating lack of opportunity for discussion of his results with any like-minded individual. As a consequence, the rich correspondence that flowed between the Cromarty mason and some of the world's most eminent naturalists assumed an enormous importance.

Much encouragement came to Miller from Dr John Malcolmson, a member of the London Geological Society. It was a far cry from the Cromarty Firth to the 'fever-marshes and tiger-jungles' of India where Malcolmson had lately carried out his own researches, but his visit to the Black Isle was to be a great help to Miller in his interpretation of the geological history of the sandstone 'where the fossils lie as thickly in some localities as herrings on our coast in the fishing season'.

Though immersed in the details of description of his fossil specimens from the fish beds, many of which were new to the scientific world of the time, Miller never lost that sense of awareness of the surrounding natural world that was the hallmark of the early naturalists. And what was more, he had the ability to convey the feeling to his readers, allowing them to accompany him on his walks by means of the word pictures he created. For example, of one of his Black Isle excursions he wrote: 'I set out . . . on a delightful morning of August 1830. The tide was falling – it had already reached the line of half-ebb; and from the Southern Sutor to the low long promontory on which the town of Cromarty is built there extended a broad belt of mingled sand-banks and pools, accumulations of boulder and shingle, and large tracts darkened with algae.' In such scenes the reader is allowed the privilege of accompanying a great naturalist on his morning walk.

There was immense satisfaction in the discoveries to be made within walking distance of Miller's home, and some flavour of this is to be found when he recounts a morning spent among the rocks at low tide on the local shore. 'I wrought on till the advancing tide came splashing over the nodules, and a powerful August sun had risen towards the middle sky; and, were I to sum up all my happier hours, the hour would not be forgotten in which I sat down on a rounded boulder of granite by the edge of the sea, when the last bed was covered, and

spread out on the beach before me the spoils of the morning.'
Clearly the writings of a man who had found a great fulfilment
in his surroundings.

Apart from the Jurassic beds at Eathie and the fish beds of
the Old Red Sandstone, there was plenty more to interest
Miller in the Black Isle landscape. The Ice Age, for example,
had created its own landforms and posed its own problems of
interpretation. The protrusions of Chanonry Ness and
Ardersier were easily enough explained in terms of colourful
local folklore, but such an explanation could hardly satisfy a
mind as enquiring as Miller's. Although open to other, more
scientific, possibilities, he acknowledged that their explanation
might lie in terms of glacial deposition, as 'a vast transverse
morain of the great valley, belonging to the same glacial age as
the lateral morains some ten or fifteen miles higher up . . .'

A question mark also hung over the exact origin of the Red
Craig cliff at Rosemarkie, a feature which Miller must have
passed on numerous occasions while walking to and from
Cromarty. 'Rosemarkie, with its long narrow valley and its red
abrupt scaurs, is chiefly interesting to the geologist for its vast
beds of the boulder clay,' he observed. 'I am acquainted with
no other locality in the kingdom where this deposit is hollowed
into ravines so profound, or presents precipices so imposing
and lofty.'

The scene which Miller describes can have changed but little
over the years. Today's visitor can still note the 'perpendicular
section of at least a hundred feet in height, barred transversely
by thin layers of sand, and scored vertically by the slow action
of the rains'. Indeed, after heavy rainfall the face of the cliff is
greatly affected by the running water, leaving black downward
streaks on the face of the soft red clay.

Deducing that this huge glacial deposit had once blocked the
mouth of the valley 'like some huge snow-wreath accumulated
athwart a frozen rivulet', Miller was much interested in the
stratified character of the deposit, but he did not fail also to
comment upon the lines of nesting burrows of the kaes or
jackdaws in the softer layers, making the cliff-face look as if it
was marked by 'shot-holes in an old tower'.

In the gullied landscape of the Dens a little further up the
valley, Miller was much intrigued by the 'hollows out of which

Hugh Miller's Cottage. The house in which the famous geologist and writer was born is in the care of the National Trust for Scotland, and is open to visitors during the summer months.

the materials of pyramids may have been taken'. It was here that he found the protruding pebbles and boulders in their red clay matrix 'forcing upon the mind the conclusion that the boulder clay is itself but an unconsolidated conglomerate of the later periods'.

Here he noted also the scratchings on the face of the rocks caused by the passage of sharp rocks embedded in the moving ice. Geologists now call them glacial striations, but Miller describes them more colourfully as being 'fretted with hieroglyphic inscriptions'. This wild and raw landscape made a deep impression on Miller's mind, and his experience of the place was clearly not confined solely to daylight hours. 'Viewed by moonlight, when the pale red of the clay where the beam falls direct is relieved by the intense shadows, these excavations of the valley of Rosemarkie form scenes of strange and ghostly wildness . . . in the solitude of the night, one almost expects to see spirits walk.'

It was not only on the large-scale and dramatic that Miller allowed his imagination to dwell. When contemplating the large boulder of the Clach Malloch exposed on the Cromarty shore at low tide, he muses on its origin as a glacial erratic, carried far from its place of origin by the moving ice and dumped at the mouth of the firth. As he ponders its past, he paints a picture of the unfolding natural history of the rock's surrounds as temperatures slowly rise when the Ice Age wanes and the climate improves. As he does so, he creates for the reader a colourful tableau of the changing Cromarty countryside through the ages. The boulder's arrival on the shore, the semi-Arctic vegetation which would have clothed the land after the melting of the ice, the forests which followed; all are vividly described. Nor is the natural and human history of the Clach Malloch itself ignored, for the boulder 'on which the tall gray heron rested moveless and ghost-like in the evenings', was also, on a more tempestuous night, the very same treacherous rock on which a ship foundered with heavy loss of life.

A present day visit to the Black Isle can be much enhanced by dipping into the neglected works of Hugh Miller. So many of the places which he so vividly describes have changed but little over the years, and familiarity with them helps bring a fine sense of the continuity of the place across the generation span. To stand below the Red Craig of Rosemarkie or look out to the Clach Malloch at Cromarty with Miller's descriptive prose familiar in the mind is an enriching experience. But perhaps the visitor's interest in the place may be literally a more down to earth one, and a search for the vividly described fish beds or for the fossil-rich shales of Eathie may bring their own satisfaction.

Whatever the source of interest in the rocks and countryside of the Black Isle, however, so much of what we know about the place today was first made known through the tireless interest of that naturalist of the old school, Hugh Miller, stonemason of Cromarty.

CHAPTER 15

Folklore and Beliefs

Enough reference has already been made to Black Isle beliefs to show that the area was once rich in local folklore. Though individual tales might lapse in the human memory, the power of superstition to fill the human mind was to persist right into present times.

For example, strange though it may seem in our scientific and sceptical age, a vague belief in mermaids persisted for a long time all around our rocky northern shores. But in the Cromarty area a couple of centuries ago the belief was strong. By tradition, the Cromarty mermaid's favourite haunt was along the rocks at the entrance to the firth. Beneath the rocky face of the North Sutor, the alluring sea creature might often be viewed in broad daylight braiding her long fair hair, and when the moonbeams scattered along the shore by night her singing would carry towards the credulous ears of the Cromarty townsfolk.

Not surprisingly, perhaps, the mermaid was often seen in the vicinity of the caves which the sea has eroded out of the hard rock around the Sutor, and it was there that a shipmaster home from sea chanced upon a fair-haired girl sitting at the water's edge. At first John Reid could not see her whole body, for she sat half in, half out of the water. He was captivated by her fair skin and long blonde hair, and when the maiden drew her lower body in from the sea, Reid was almost blinded by the reflected brilliance of her scaly tail. The seafarer had come face-to-face with none other than the mermaid of the rocks!

The strange sea creature was equally startled by the sudden human appearance. Uttering a piercing shriek, she tried to make for the shore, but Reid threw his strong arms around her, and there could be no escape. When the mermaid realised that she was held fast, she spoke in a voice that made her captor's blood run cold. 'Man, what with me?' the creature asked.

'Wishes three' was Reid's reply.

His three dearest wishes thus divulged, Reid let go of the

mermaid who, with that same pent-up power which a salmon possesses in its tail, thrust herself off the rock and disappeared slowly into the green depths. In due time, the shipmaster's wishes were to be granted, but the mermaid was seen no more along the Cromarty shore.

So ran Hugh Miller's tale of the mermaid of Cromarty. But not many miles across the outer firth, the story was to have an intriguing parallel. In the year 1814, it was widely reported that two Banffshire fishermen chanced upon a long-haired, ample-breasted mermaid at sea. The tale was told immediately on their return to a local schoolmaster who had no cause to question their strange story. But an even stranger thing was that the creature was not alone. Her strange, flat-nosed, curly-haired companion was clearly a merman, suggesting, presumably, that there might be a whole race of these intriguing creatures of the deep living around the firths.

But if there was, or is, then why are they not seen these days? The answer perhaps is that they may be. About ten years ago a lady in the Black Isle told the writer of a place where a mermaid had been seen on the rocks only a generation or two before. Such, it seems, is the enduring power of Black Isle folk belief.

Many corners of the Black Isle had their own supernatural associations. The cave at the foot of Craigiehowe near Munlochy Bay has been a shelter for wild goats and travelling folk in more recent times, but local legend identified it as the temporary resting place of a band of Celtic warriors awaiting a rousing trumpet blast that would stir them into action once more. In days long gone, local farmers were prepared to take no chances, blocking up the entrance to the cave in the belief that if their sheep and goats strayed into its dark recesses they would never be seen again.

High above rocky Craigiehowe lies little Loch Lundie, the largest water body on the Black Isle. It is now frequented only by anglers, but once it was the haunt of a 'tairbh uisghe' or water bull. One can readily imagine how, in times gone by, the churning of the water by the wind might be interpreted in believers' ears as the cavortions of the dreaded water beast.

In a less sophisticated age, quite ordinary objects and happenings in the world of nature could be imbued with

The rocky shore at McFarquhar's Bed near Cromarty. Belief in mermaids along this shore was once strong in the area.

strange powers. The drip of water from the roof of the Craigiehowe cave was a well-known cure for deafness and earache, the sufferer tilting his head to allow the icy cold drips to penetrate his ear. The parish minister of the late eighteenth century was not convinced, however, asserting that 'In my opinion this must be owing to the cold and piercing quality of the water forcing its way through the obstruction of the ear'. Perhaps in days before doctors' ear syringes, the force of the icy drip falling from the cave roof was sufficient to dislodge impacted ear wax, thereby effecting an instant improvement in hearing!

There are other Black Isle dropping caves. The best known lies a little distance along the rocky shore from Cromarty. Its mouth was once a haunt of the Cromarty mermaid, and in days long gone, fishermen told how, when darkness fell about the South Sutor, an eerie blue light glowed from its entrance. However, it was not the drips from the roof of this cave that had curative properties but the bubbling water of a natural spring a short distance away. According to local belief, this issue of pure water, known locally as Fiddler's Well, had a most unusual origin.

In an age when the scourge of consumption (tuberculosis) claimed many an unfulfilled life, two young Cromarty men were struck down by the disease at the same time. They had been the best of friends, but death was now set to divide them. The survivor, whose surname was Fiddler, saw his friend to the grave, and appeared certain to follow soon afterwards.

Then a curious thing happened. After a night of fevered visions of death, Fiddler dreamed of a sunny sea-shore. In his delirium a voice said 'Go on, Willie; I shall meet you at Stormy'. The voice seemed to be that of the friend whom he had seen borne to the churchyard only hours before, and the place a sea-washed rock in the vicinity.

Still in his dream Fiddler sought out the spot to which he had been instructed to go, but though he waited long enough for his departed companion to appear, he had only the sound of the sea for a companion. Distraught at the loss of his friend, Fiddler broke down. In the midst of his grief he became aware of the hum of a bumble bee. At first he tried to brush the persistent insect away from his head, but then its buzzing seemed to form into words. 'Dig, Willie, and drink!' the insect droned, and Willie responded by scraping at the ground with his bare hands. Suddenly, a spring of clearest water gushed from the bank, and when it did so the bee disappeared as mysteriously as it had come.

Before he had a chance to drink from the well, Fiddler's dream began to fade, to be replaced by the reality of his sickroom walls around him. But the memory stayed vividly with him, and rising from his bed he made his way to the spot where the bee had droned its message. Digging into the very same place, water sprang from the ground, pure, clear water which was to effect a miraculous cure. For generations afterwards, local folk believed in the efficacy of the well as a cure for all manner of bodily ills, though the healing waters had to be quaffed in the morning, just as in Willie Fiddler's prophetic dream.

Again, this is one of Hugh Miller's intriguing tales of the Cromarty district. J.M. McPherson, in his *Primitive Beliefs of the North-east of Scotland* suggested that to the bee was attached a certain sanctity. While it appeared to be the form in which Willie Fiddler's late companion had returned, there may have been in the drone of the bee some last echo of an old folk belief. Perhaps the bee that buzzed around Fiddler's Well may have been the embodiment of the spirit of the unseen spring, just as other forms of animal life elsewhere held the same kind of guardian role.

Much better known last century, when it attracted the attention of a stream of curious visitors, is a natural spring that issues out of the rock above Munlochy Bay. This, the Craiguck Well, has been resorted to as a source of healing for many generations, and even today there is a lingering belief in its power to cure. Perhaps Craiguck Well would have received less attention had it not been a clootie (rag) well, that is to say visitors drinking of its waters leave a small piece of cloth tied to one of the surrounding branches. The morning of the first Sunday in May is the time to visit this well, and even today it still attracts a small stream of visitors.

Craiguck Well is dedicated to St Bennet whose name appears in other local place-names. Finding a well-entrenched pagan custom surrounding well worship, the early church seemed to have attempted to incorporate it into the new religion by dedicating the various wells to Christian saints.

The continued entwining of strands of the two faiths surprised visitors to the area. In his fascinating book *The Past in the Present* Sir Arthur Mitchell wrote in 1862 of his astonishment at finding the large briar bush beside the well draped with threads and rags left behind by drinkers at the spring. 'It was not without astonishment,' he observed, 'that, in so Protestant a part of Protestant Scotland as the parish of Avoch, I found the bush above Craiguck Well, when I visited it last summer literally covered with such offerings'.

Before sunrise on the appointed morning, Mitchell was surprised to find that 'Young and old, hale and hearty, as well as sick and diseased, thronged to it as to a fair'. For the healthy there was a belief in the health-giving properties of the water. For the sick, belief in its curative power was doubtless an encouragement in an age when medical science offered far less hope than it does today. In the leaving of the rag by a sick person, there was also incorporated the old belief that the disease might pass to the sacred tree in the act of transferring a piece of garment to its branches.

Taking the waters at the well involved a ritual in which the visitor spilled some water three times on the ground and crossed himself before fixing a rag to the bush. Only then was it propitious to drink from the waters.

The Brahan Seer (see below), whose prophetic utterings were well respected in the Black Isle, is said to have given a kind of formula for ascertaining the likelihood of success following a well visit. 'Whoever he be that drinketh ... if suffering from any disease, shall by placing two pieces of straw or wood on the surface, ascertain whether he will recover or not. If he is to recover, the straws will whirl round in opposite directions; if he is to die soon, they will remain stationary.'

Better known to visitors than Craiguck is another spring which gushes into a trough on the main road from Dingwall, just outside the village of Munlochy. In recent times St Boniface's Well has become a stopping place on the tourist trail through the Black Isle, and rags are hung around it at any time of the year, not just on the first Sunday in May. In fact, few visitors are aware of the sacred origins of any of the old wells in

Clootie Well near Munlochy. The practice of fixing rags to the bushes surrounding the well shows no signs of dying out, though most are now placed there by visitors unfamiliar with the well's ancient and holy origin.

the Highlands today, and St Boniface's well has simply taken on the function of a wishing well. In the past, a silver coin was regarded as an appropriate offering.

Unfortunately, with the replacement of cotton and linen by almost indestructable synthetic fibres, the rags do not disintegrate, and the result is a bizarre accumulation, ranging from men's ties to ladies' tights festooning the branches. The decline of a disease as the fibres of the transferred rag rotted away would doubtless be a much slower process today!

In the damp roadside shade, a covering of green algae has spread over the hanging materials, giving the rags an unsavoury appearance. Those who live in its vicinity and who might be sceptics in the matter of the power of the well seem, however, to retain enough superstition to restrain them from putting a match to the eyesore and thus removing what is locally regarded as a blot on the Black Isle landscape!

It would be strange indeed if there was no local tradition of witchcraft in the Black Isle, since belief in this aspect of the supernatural was once so widespread. A stone still standing on the Fortrose and Rosemarkie golf course marks the supposed place of a witch's fiery execution, and not far away, a lump of grey stone at Chanonry Point commemorates the time when a famous Highland seer went up in a grisly plume of smoke as the price of his supernatural powers, but more of him anon.

In the middle of the seventeenth century four unfortunate women from the district of Ferintosh were branded as witches and taken off to be 'pricked', in the cruel way of the time, to establish their guilt or otherwise. History does not record the ultimate fate of the Ferintosh women after they had been subjected to the degradation of stripping and the insertion of pins into their naked flesh.

Defenceless wild creatures might be regarded as witches in disguise. Hares were favourite candidates for this curious belief, and suspicions lurked long in people's minds whenever there was a close encounter with one of these large-eyed beasts of the Black Isle countryside.

At the Muir of Ord market in November 1877, for example, a hare appeared on the scene, pursued by the numerous collie dogs which were gathered there. As a local newspaper reported, 'A decent looking woman . . . lifted up her hands and exclaimed in Gaelic 'Cha neil teagaibh san bith nach i sid aon dhe ban bhuidhseach na Toiseachd.' ('There can be no doubt but that the animal is one of the old Ferintosh witches . . . You'll see this is to be a bad market'.)

Witchcraft, could only survive as long as human belief persisted in it. But so long as it did, it might be applied with devastating effect. For example, the placing of a clay effigy in a stream to waste away in the current's flow, was a time-honoured method of dealing with an enemy. For as long as there was a community awareness that such things might be going on, there were plenty of people around who would vouch for the efficacy of the method, and even the clergy might be counted among their ranks as one true story from a Black Isle parish shows.

Around the middle of the eighteenth century, the minister of Killearnan was much troubled by a tendency to drop off to sleep. While it was one thing in an age of interminable sermons for the congregation to 'drop off', the tendency for the minister to do the same was becoming something of an embarrassment. The minister himself was disposed to believe that he had been bewitched, and two local women were regarded as prime suspects. Rumour had it that they had made a clay effigy of the minister and stuck pins into it. Hardly surprisingly in the circumstances, the minister was tempted to ascribe the pains he was feeling at the time to the power of applied witchcraft.

While such on-goings were perhaps not uncommon for the times in which they occurred, what is surprising is the span of time such beliefs covered. As late as 1878, the *Ross-shire Journal* reported the finding of just such an effigy in a burn to the west side of the Black Isle.

It was no uncommon thing for supernatural spirits to have a watery association. Because of local belief, the Bodach's Bridge over the burn at Newhall was no place for the faint-hearted on a foul night. Towards the latter part of the eighteenth century, there lived in its vicinity an old man who was a great believer in the supernatural. Late one evening, while crossing the bridge, he came face-to-face with a lady whom he did not recognise.

She was somewhat unconventionally dressed for such a setting, for she wore a brown silk gown and high-heeled shoes. She said she had a message for him, but it was one which the old man would rather not have heard. She had come to tell him that he was fated to die on a certain day. As can be imagined, the bodach was greatly troubled, but far from accepting his neighbours' advice to dismiss the matter as mere hallucination, he brooded on the strange lady's message. Needless to say, he worried himself into an early grave, expiring on the very day the strange lady had predicted.

A curious illustration of the survival of superstitious belief concerns an occurrence in the autumn of 1884. It seems that rumour spread like wildfire around Fortrose that someone had dreamed of an impending disaster for one of the small steamers which plied between the Black Isle and Inverness. It happened to be the day of a big feeing market in the Highland capital, and large numbers of people had gathered to make the crossing of the firth to attend it. Yet, rather than risk disaster, the great majority opted to go round to Inverness by road, giving themselves a time-consuming detour of around twenty miles and the local newspaper a subject of comment for its columns.

Foreknowledge of the future through the power of a seer has been a feature of Highland folklife for countless generations, and continues to be so to this very day. The subject has been well discussed by Black Isle writer Elizabeth Sutherland in her book *Ravens and Black Rain*.

Best known of all Highland seers, was Coinneach Odhar, dun-coloured Kenneth Mackenzie. Because of his association with the family of the Seaforth Mackenzies at Brahan, an estate a short distance to the west of the Black Isle, Coinneach was dubbed the 'Brahan Seer' by a writer last century, and the name has stuck. However, Elizabeth Sutherland has pointed to the importance of his Gaelic style, Fiosaiche, meaning a soothsayer, augur, or sorcerer.

History has shown that some of Coinneach's predictions came to have an uncanny fulfilment. For example, he foresaw the day when full-rigged ships would sail round the back of Tomnahurich Hill in Inverness. In due course, the creation of Telford's Caledonian Canal which passed round behind the hill was regarded both as an engineering achievement and as a prophetic fulfilment. The curious glacial mound of Tomnahurich and the exit lock of the canal which skirts it may be clearly seen from the Kessock Bridge when approaching the Black Isle.

Of all Coinneach's prophecies, however, one stands out above all others both for its associations with the Black Isle and for the strangeness of its fulfilment. It will be recalled from a previous chapter that the red sandstone walls of the cathedral of Chanonry are lined with the memorial tablets of the Seaforth Mackenzies. In the annals of Highland belief, their fate has been intimately tied to that of Coinneach Odhar.

Tradition tells the tale this way. Kenneth, third Earl of Seaforth was away in France on some important matter of business. His wife, the Countess Isabella, was at home at Brahan Castle, anxious for her husband's return. Pestering Coinneach for some explanation of the Earl's over-long stay, the Countess eventually was given more than she bargained for. Coinneach informed her that her husband was dallying in the company of a French lady, and in the circumstances

Sunrise behind the Brahan Seer's memorial stone at Chanonry Point, an atmospheric place where the strands of past and present are closely interwoven.

presumably in no hurry to return to Scotland.

The Countess was furious both at the news and at what she regarded as her humiliation by Coinneach in front of others. At once Isabella had him seized and condemned to a horrible death by burning in a barrel of tar on Chanonry Ness. But the victim of the Countess's ire had not yet finished. Before a torch was put to his volatile funeral pyre, he uttered the prophesy which foresaw the demise of the House of Seaforth.

The way in which local belief saw the fulfilment of the Seer's gloomy prophecies is now a celebrated legend. Coinneach foresaw the last clan chief, both deaf and dumb, following his sons to the grave. In fact, the last chief died in the early 19th century, his hearing permanently impaired by an illness and his will to speak weakened by the trauma of seeing his four sons die, one after the other.

The prophecy also had a reference to a 'white-coifed lass' who would kill her sister. On the death of the chief, the clan lands passed to his eldest daughter who was widow of Admiral Sir Samuel Hood. In a tragic accident, marked by a memorial beside the main road on the Brahan lands near Moy bridge, she was to be the cause of her younger sister's death in a carriage accident, hence fulfiling yet another part of the fateful prediction.

The cold marble slabs on the walls of the Cathedral of Chanonry therefore now stand as a stark memorial to a family whose long-term fate is popularly said to have been sealed when its path was crossed by that of Coinneach Odhar Fiosaiche.

In a strange, but perhaps not unexpected way, it might be said that Coinneach Odhar continues to haunt the Black Isle to this day. When a wedding took place in the ruined cathedral in the 1970s, word quickly spread around Fortrose that Coinneach had prophesied that it would be followed by many deaths in the Chanonry. As it happened, there did follow a greater than normal number of deaths in the local community, but the fact was that this 'prophesy' was unknown before the happening.

Of Coinneach's exact burning place, no reminder now remains. A marking slab of rock was said once to exist somewhere close to Chanonry Point, but is now lost to sight. Yet such is the place of Coinneach Odhar in the Black Isle's past and in its folk belief, that the former Fortrose Town Council arranged for a memorial stone to be set up near the Lighthouse. Pupils of Fortrose Academy cast the inscribed plaque on the boulder's side, and its presence at a popular summer parking spot is the means of setting many visitors on the trail of this shadowy character from the past.

Indeed, in the quietness of a winter morning when the eerie calls of flighting divers pierce the frosty air, and the memorial stone is starkly silhouetted against the lightening sky, the Black Isle's past and present seem closely interwoven in this atmospheric place which once echoed to the crackle of a seer's burning.

Further Reading

Anson, P. – *Fishing Boats and Fisher Folk* (Dent, 1971)

Duncan, U.K. – *Flora of Easter Ross* (Botanical Society of Edinburgh, 1980)

Fawcett, R. & Breeze, D.J. – *Beauly Priory and Fortrose Cathedral* (HMSO, 1987)

Inverness Field Club – *The Moray Firth Area Geological Studies* (Inverness Field Club, 1977)

Mackenzie, A. – *Prophecies of the Brahan Seer* (Aeneas Mackay, 1924)

Marshall, E. – *The Black Isle. A Portrait of the Past* (Protheroe, Fortrose, 1973)

Mather, A.S. (Ed.) – *The County of Ross and Cromarty. Third Statistical Account of Scotland* (Scottish Academic Press, 1987)

Meldrum, E. *The Black Isle. Local History and Archaeology Guidebook No.3* (Author, 1979)

Miller, H. – *My Schools and Schoolmasters* (Nimmo, 1870)
  – *Scenes and Legends of the North of Scotland* (Nimmo, 1878)
  – *The Cruise of the Betsey* with *Rambles of a Geologist* (Nimmo, Hay & Mitchell, 1889)
  – *The Old Red Sandstone* (Nimmo, Hay & Mitchell, 1892)

Mowat, I.R.M. – *Easter Ross. The Double Frontier* (John Donald, 1981)

Romans, J.C.C. – *The Soils of the Black Isle* (The Macaulay Institute for Soil Research, 1985)

'St Duthac' – *Fortrose: A Garden City by the Sea* (Gilmour & Lawrence, 1912)

Sutherland, D.K. – *Fisherlore of Avoch* (Author, 1986)

Sutherland, E. – *Ravens and Black Rain* (Constable, 1985)

Watson, W.J. – *Place-names of Ross & Cromarty* (Ross & Cromarty Heritage Society reprint, 1976)
  – *Ross & Cromarty* (Cambridge University Press, 1924)

Index